2X4 Projects for Outdoor Living

2X4 Projects for Outdoor Living

S T E V I E H E N D E R S O N
A N D M A R K B A L D W I N

LARK BOOKS

A Division of Sterling Publishing Co., Inc.
New York

Editor: Laura Dover Doran
Book and Cover Design: Dana Irwin
Photostylist: Chris Bryant
Photographer: Evan Bracken
Illustrator: Todd Jarrett
Editorial Assistance: Catharine Sutherland
Production Assistance: Hannes Charen

Library of Congress Cataloging-in-Publication Data

Henderson, Stevie, 1943-
    2X4 projects for outdoor living/ Stevie Henderson and Mark Baldwin.
        p.   cm.
    Includes index.
    ISBN 1-57990-164-6 (pbk.)
    1. Outdoor furniture. 2. Furniture making. 3. Garden ornaments and furniture--Design
and construction. I. Title: Two by four projects for outdoor living. II. Baldwin, Mark.
III. Title.

TT197.5.09 H45 2000
684.1'8--dc21

10 9 8 7 6 5 4 3

Published by Lark Books, a division of
Sterling Publishing Co., Inc.
387 Park Avenue South, New York, N.Y. 10016

Distributed in Canada by Sterling Publishing,
c/o Canadian Manda Group, One Atlantic Ave., Suite 105
Toronto, Ontario, Canada M6K 3E7

Distributed in Australia by Capricorn Link (Australia) Pty Ltd.,
P.O. Box 704, Windsor, NSW 2756 Australia

Distributed in the U.K. by:
Guild of Master Craftsman Publications Ltd.
Castle Place 166 High Street, Lewes, East Sussex, England, BN7 1XU
Tel: (+ 44) 1273 477374 Fax: (+ 44) 1273 478606
Email: pubs@thegmcgroup.com, Web: www.gmcpublications.com

If you have questions or comments about this book, please contact:
Lark Books, 50 College St., Asheville, NC 28801, (828) 253-0467

C O N T E N T S

More and more we find ourselves living out-of-doors. In years past, we might have grilled burgers on Saturday afternoon or picnicked during the day on Sunday, but now we find ourselves sitting on the deck with friends on a weeknight and holding most of our parties in the backyard. Perhaps it is a return to the days when grandma and grandpa sat on the front porch and visited with neighbors, or perhaps today we cherish a more casual way of living. Whatever the reason, our backyards have become extended living areas.

To make our new living area "liveable" requires a whole new list of desirable additions to the yard and garden. And those additions are very costly if you purchase them in specialty stores. Not having shopped for outdoor furniture and fixtures in a number of years, we were appalled at the prices for tables, swings, deck chairs, and fountains. Rather than settle for four plastic chairs and a matching plastic table, we decided to build our outdoor living furniture and fixtures. We are thrilled with the results. Not only did we save money, but our new outdoor rooms are filled with practical and attractive pieces that fit our outdoor living lifestyle.

Even if you have never picked up a hammer and nails, this book is for you. We have simplified the construction of every project with the beginner in mind. Browse through the book, pick out a project, and read through the instructions. We will bet you'll agree that you can do it. There is something for everyone, and even the largest projects, such as the Mini Gazebo, will take just a couple of weekends to complete. Build a small project to get started, and, after that success, you'll be tackling everything in the book.

Happy outdoor living!

MATERIALS

Adhesives

Since this book deals with exterior projects that will be exposed to the weather much of the time, a weatherproof glue is mandatory. Ordinary interior glue will dissolve when exposed to the elements. The easiest glue to use is an exterior-formulated version of ordinary straw-colored carpenter's glue. Look for the words "exterior use" on the container. You may also use the more costly two-part resorcinol, though it takes about 12 hours to set and at least another 12 hours to cure completely.

Don't overdo the amount of glue you use. If too much is applied, the glue will be squeezed out of the joint and drip all over your project when pressure is applied. Just apply a small ribbon of glue down the center of one surface, then rub the adjoining surface against the ribbon to distribute the glue evenly. Your objective is to coat both surfaces with a uniform, thin coating. If you do encounter drips, wipe them off quickly with a damp cloth. It is easy to do at the moment, but if you let the glue dry, it can be very difficult to remove. If it dries, it will have to be sanded off, since it will not accept most stains.

Fasteners

The projects in this book are designed for exterior use, so any fastener you use to construct them must also be weatherproof—or at least weather resistant. There are several different kinds of materials and coatings that make a nail or screw suitable for exterior use. The basic rule is that the longer the coating or material is expected to last, the more you can expect to pay for it.

The most popular choices for nails and screws used for outdoor woodworking are described below.

Galvanized fasteners are coated with zinc, are inexpensive, and are the most widely used type of coated fastener. Over time, they may stain redwood and cedar, and corrode in pressure-treated wood.

Anodized fasteners are roughly equivalent to galvanized in quality and performance.

Zinc-plated fasteners are somewhat more weather resistant but difficult to find outside specialty stores.

Brass fasteners are lovely to look at and resistant to weather but lack strength.

Stainless steel fasteners are highly resistant to corrosion and extremely strong but extremely expensive.

Another note about galvanized products: It may be worth the extra trouble to look for what are known as "hot-dipped" or mechanically galvanized nails or screws rather than the somewhat less-expensive products that use an electrical plating technique. The dipping process more effectively deposits zinc on the surface of the metal.

Ultimately, we tend to match the quality of the fasteners we choose to the quality of the wood. For example, if you are building a project out of expensive teak, it makes sense to purchase stainless steel screws. If you are using inexpensive pressure-treated pine, galvanized decking screws are probably the logical choice.

NAILS

Although there are many different types of nails (common, large flathead, duplex head, oval head, and so forth),

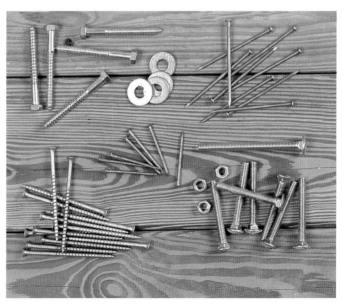

An assortment of nails, screws, brads, washers, and nuts

the one most commonly used in woodworking is a *finish nail*. It has a much smaller head than the common nail, making it easy to recess below the surface of the wood, or countersink. The small hole remaining on the surface is easily concealed with wood filler.

Nail sizes are designated by "penny" (abbreviated as "d"). Penny size directly corresponds to length, although the diameter is larger for longer nails. They range in length from 1 inch to 6 inches. Confused? To determine the penny size of a particular nail length, the following method works well for lengths up to 3 inches (10d). Take the length of the nail you need, subtract ½ inch, and multiply by four. For example, if you need a 2½-inch nail, subtract ½ inch, and multiply by four. What you need is

Penny Size	Length
2d	1"
3d	1¼"
4d	1½"
5d	1¾"
6d	2"
7d	2¼"
8d	2½"
9d	2¾"
10d	3"
12d	3¼"
16d	3½"
20d	4"

an 8-penny nail (8d). Some of the more commonly used nail sizes are listed above.

As a general rule, when joining two pieces of wood, use a nail length that will provide the greatest amount of holding power without penetrating the opposite surface. For example, if you are joining two 1 x 4s, each piece of wood is ¾ inch thick—a total of 1½ inches of wood. To maximize your holding power, you should choose a 1¼-inch nail.

Nails driven in at an angle provide more holding power than those that are driven straight into the work. *Toenailing* refers to the process of driving a nail into the wood at an extreme angle to secure two pieces together.

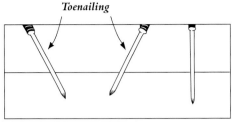

Toenailing

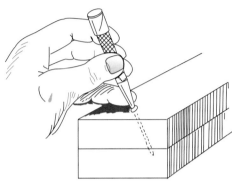

The most difficult part of toenailing comes when the nail is nearly all the way into the wood and only the head and a bit of the shank are visible. To avoid making hammer marks on your wood, hammer the nail into the piece until the head is still slightly above the surface. Then use a nail set to finish the job and countersink the nail.

In fact, the best way to prevent hammer marks on all of your work is to use a nail set. The trick to using a nail set effectively is to hold it in the proper manner. It should be steadied with the hand by gripping it firmly with all four fingers and your thumb. Rest your little finger on the surface of the wood for added stability.

If you are working with hardwood, a very narrow piece of softwood, or any wood that has a tendency to split when you nail into it, it is wise to predrill the nail hole. Choose a drill bit that is just barely smaller than the diameter of the nail, and drill a pilot hole about two-thirds the length of the nail.

BRADS

Wire brads are used for attaching trim or for very small projects. They are just a smaller and thinner version of finish nails. They are designated in length in inches and wire gauge numbers from 11 to 0. The lower the gauge number, the larger the diameter.

SCREWS

The advantage of screws over nails is their holding power and the fact that (when used without glue) they can be removed easily at a later date. Their disadvantage is that they are not as easy to insert. Almost all of the projects in the book use screws in the construction.

As with nails, there are many kinds of screws. The one most often used in woodworking is a flathead Phillips screw. As the name implies, it has a flat head that can be countersunk below the surface. It is most often labeled as a "drywall screw" and can be driven with a power drill.

Screws are designated by length and diameter. In general, as with nails, you want to use the longest screw possible that will not penetrate the opposite surface. The diameter of a screw is described by its gauge number. Common sizes range from #2 to #16, with larger diameters having higher gauge numbers.

When you are working on very soft wood, it is possi-

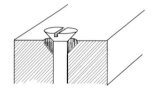

Wood Plug

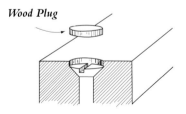

ble to countersink a screw simply by driving it with a power drill. However, the resulting surface hole may be covered only by using wood filler. An alternate method is to predrill the screw hole and insert a wood plug over the top of the countersunk screw head.

Predrilling is normally a two-step operation. First drill the larger, countersunk portion deep enough and at a

diameter just slightly larger than the diameter of the screw head (or the depth and diameter to accommodate the screw and the wood plug you are using). Then drill the pilot hole in the center of the larger hole, using a drill bit the same diameter as the solid portion of the screw (minus the threads). If you use the same size screws on a regular basis, you may wish to invest in a combination pilot-countersink bit for your drill, which will perform both operations at the same time.

You can purchase wood plugs, or you can cut your own. It is easy to slice a wooden dowel rod into many wood plugs. The only disadvantage to this plug is that it will show the end grain and will be visible if you stain the wood. The alternative is to cut your own plugs using a plug cutter, but that method requires a drill press.

Screws can be inserted at an angle, the same way that nails are, to toenail two pieces of wood together. After some practice, you will be able to start a screw at any angle with very little or no effort. If you find it difficult, simply use a drill or a screw starter to begin your screw hole.

Although you do not want to add so many screws to your project that the metal outweighs the wood, do not be stingy with them. If there is the slightest chance that the joint could be shaky, add a couple of extra screws. Remember that the project you are making will probably be subjected to several moves over the course of the years—either to a different room or a different house—which will place additional strain on the joints.

Wood

The two basic classifications of wood are softwood and hardwood. As the name implies, softwood is usually softer and therefore easier to work with than hardwood. It is also much less expensive. Because of this, softwood is usually a good choice for beginning woodworkers. We built all of the projects in this book with softwood, but, of course, they can be built with hardwood. We have specified pine in the instructions, but use whatever softwood is most plentiful (and least expensive) in your area.

Softwood is cut from coniferous trees (evergreens)

such as pine, redwood, and cedar. Hardwood comes from deciduous trees such as maple, cherry, and walnut, which shed their leaves each year.

Because these projects are designed for outdoor use (which does not mean you *have* to use them outdoors), you will most likely want to use wood that will stand up to life in the great outdoors. Damp weather, insects, and fungi cause wood to deteriorate. Heartwood, the dense, dead wood from the inner core of a tree, repels moisture and insects far more effectively than the sapwood that surrounds it. However, this core wood takes years to develop, and most old-growth trees were harvested years ago. Today, most commercial lumber consists of second-growth timber that lacks any substantial amount of heartwood.

Some species are naturally resistant to decay and insects. They include white cedar, redwood, black locust, cypress, hemlock, and oak. Douglas fir and Southern yellow pine, although they are not as resistant to damage, are good choices for outdoor projects. They are reasonably priced, hard, and durable. They also do well when chemically treated.

You can use untreated pine for smaller projects, as long as the lumber is thoroughly sealed, painted, and sealed again. If the piece you are building will be exposed to the elements for any length of time, we recommend that you use a treated pine.

TREATED WOOD

There are two general categories of preservatives used to treat wood: oils, such as creosote and pentachlorophenol solutions in petroleum, and chemical salts that are applied as waterborne solutions. The lumber you purchase will probably be treated with the second method, and is known as pressure-treated, or "PT," wood. The name is apt, as the preservatives are forced under pressure into the cells of the wood to protect it from destructive organisms. Lumber treated in this way will last five to 10 times longer than untreated lumber.

Pressure-treated lumber is classified by how it will be used: above ground or in contact with the ground. If any portion of the project will come in contact with the ground, use the latter classification, even though it is more expensive. Just to make things more complicated, there is also a difference between pressure-treated wood used for decks and buildings and pressure-treated wood used for general purposes. This information should be printed on a tag stapled to the end grain of the lumber you buy. If not, ask the salesperson to help you determine whether you are buying the best treated lumber for your needs. Ratings may simply be LP-2 for above-ground use and LP-22 for below-ground use. If you plan to build a trellis and place it directly on the lawn, we recommend that you purchase below-ground treated wood.

Please keep in mind that there are chemicals in treated lumber. Always wear a dust mask when you cut treated lumber. Never burn treated-wood scraps. And, if you are concerned about possible skin sensitivities to treated lumber, you may want to wear leather gloves. After handling treated lumber, be sure to wash your hands before eating, and wash your work clothes separately from other laundry.

The ultimate choice of wood will probably be driven by your budget. For each of the materials required for exterior projects, the cost goes up relative to its ability to withstand the onslaught of Mother Nature. Untreated pine will work when correctly finished and placed in a protected area; above-ground treated pine will be fine for projects placed on a patio or deck; and below-ground treated pine will work for projects placed directly on the ground. Moving up in expense, redwood or cypress work well for all projects and can be placed directly on the ground.

SOFTWOOD

Softwood is sold in most building supply stores in dimensional sizes—1 x 4s, 2 x 4s, and so forth. And it is sold in specific foot lengths. So you can buy a 1 x 4 x 6, or a 1 x 4 x 8, or a 1 x 4 x 10, and so forth. This would seem to make it simple. And it would be if a 1 x 4 was actually 1 inch thick and 4 inches wide. But such is not the case. Apparently the sawmills, lumberyards, and building supply stores have conspired in a huge plot to confuse us, because a 1 x 4 is actually ¾ inch thick and 3½ inches wide. There is a reason for this. When the board was cut originally, it was 1 inch

Nominal Size	Actual Dimensions
1 x 1	¾" x ¾"
1 x 2	¾" x 1½"
1 x 3	¾" x 2½"
1 x 4	¾" x 3½"
1 x 6	¾" x 5½"
1 x 8	¾" x 7¼"
1 x 10	¾" x 9¼"
1 x 12	¾" x 11¼"
2 x 2	1½" x 1½"
2 x 4	1½" x 3½"
2 x 6	1½" x 5½"
2 x 8	1½" x 7¼"
2 x 10	1½" x 9¼"
2 x 12	1½" x 11¼"
4 x 4	3½" x 3½"
4 x 6	3½" x 3½"
6 x 6	5½" x 5½"
8 x 8	7½" x 7½"
5/4 deck boards	1¼" x 5¾"

thick and 4 inches wide. But when it is surfaced on all four sides, its actual dimensions are less. Listed above are the nominal sizes and the actual dimensions.

Softwood is also graded according to its quality. And, as with anything else, the better the quality, the higher the price. Do not buy a better quality than you need for the project you are building. A few imperfections may even make your project look more rustic (if that is the look you are after). The softwood grades are as follows.

COMMON GRADES

No. 1 common contains knots and a few imperfections but should have no knotholes.

No. 2 common is free of knotholes but contains some knots.

No. 3 common contains larger knots and small knotholes.

No. 4 common is used for construction only and contains large knotholes.

No. 5 common is the lowest grade of lumber and is used only when strength and appearance are not important.

SELECT GRADES

B and better (or 1 and 2 clear) are the best and most expensive grades used for the finest furniture projects.

C select may have a few small blemishes.

D select is the lowest quality of the better board grades. It has imperfections that can be concealed with paint.

Clear boards (those that are nearly free of imperfections) come from the center section (heartwood) of the tree, and *sapwood* (wood that have more knots and other flaws) comes from the outer sections.

Consider the type of finish that you want to apply to the completed project. If you plan to stain the finished piece, pay particular attention to the grain of the wood, and choose boards that have fewer imperfections and similar grain patterns. If you are going to paint the finished piece, you can purchase a lower grade of wood and cover the defects with wood filler and paint.

No matter what grade you purchase, you should inspect each and every board for defects and imperfections. A little extra inspection time in the store will save you hours of frustration later and will be well worth the effort. Some stores will not allow you to hand-select individual boards—take your business elsewhere. Although it is possible (but extremely time-consuming) to correct some defects in wood, it is simply easier to purchase blemish-free boards in the first place. There is no point in buying wood that is unusable, no matter how cheap the price.

Many large building supply stores purchase their wood from different suppliers, and that means that even in the same bin at the same store, the board widths may vary slightly. On the surface (no pun intended), that may not seem like a big deal. But even a difference of ¹⁄₆₄th of an inch in width between two boards will mean that your project will not fit together correctly. So when you purchase wood for a specific project, place the boards together to make certain that they are all exactly the same width.

While you are checking, examine the board for warping and/or bowing. Warpage occurs over the length of the board, and bowing occurs across the width of the board. If you will be cutting only very short pieces of wood and

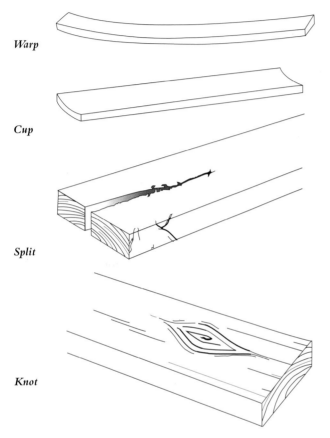

Warp

Cup

Split

Knot

the warpage is very slight, it probably will not affect your finished project. But if you need longer lengths, search until you find boards that are straight along the entire length. A good method to check for warping or bowing before you buy is to place one end of the board on the floor, and look down its length. Then turn the board and look down the edge. Your own eye is the best test.

Also check for knots. Small, tight knots are usually okay—especially for furniture that you plan to paint. But large knots may become a problem, as they are tough to cut through and also may fall out, leaving you with an unattractive hole in your finished project. Some imperfections can simply be eliminated. If a board is otherwise acceptable, but has a knothole on the end, it is easy

enough to simply cut it off. But be sure to purchase extra material to compensate for the loss.

Avoid buying boards that contain splits. Splits have a nasty habit of growing lengthwise, ultimately resulting in two narrow and unusable boards. If the split occurs only at one end, you can cut it off; but again, allow extra material for the waste.

SELECTING WOOD

For purposes of clarity, this book refers to each surface of a board by a specific name. The broadest part of the board is called a *face*, and the narrow surface along the length of the board is an *edge*. The *ends*, as the name suggests, are the smallest surfaces occurring on the extremities of each board.

It will be time well spent to read through the instructions and cutting list of an individual project before shopping for your materials. Each materials list specifies the total number of linear feet of a particular wood required to make the project. So if the total linear feet required is 40 feet, you can purchase five 8-foot lengths, four 10-foot lengths, and so on. When you arrive at the lumberyard or store, you may find that the 8-foot lengths of wood are of lesser quality than the 6-foot lengths. So you could then buy seven 6-foot lengths and have a little left over. But you must first check to make certain that no single piece required by the project is over 6-feet long.

It is also wise to keep transportation abilities in mind. If you own (or can borrow) a pickup truck to transport your materials, board lengths are not a factor. But it is pretty difficult to get a 12-foot length of wood into a Corvette for the trip home. Most building supply stores will be happy to give you one free cut on an individual piece of lumber, but some charge a fee.

Unless you have chosen a very expensive wood to build your project, it makes sense to slightly overbuy your materials. That way if you do make a mistake, you have a "reserve" board to bail you out. Returning to the store for just one more board is frustrating, time-consuming, and (depending upon how far you have to drive) sometimes more expensive than if you had purchased an extra one on the original trip. We have built some overage into the materials list to accommodate squaring-off the piece and allowing for the width of saw cuts.

HARDWOOD

You can also use hardwood to build any of the projects in this book. Hardwood, as the name implies, will resist dents and scratches much better than softwood. The downside is that it is more difficult to work with and is extremely expensive.

If you decide to use a hardwood for your project, it will take some calculating on your part, since hardwood is normally sold in random widths and lengths. Each board is cut from the log as wide and as long as possible. Consequently, hardwood is sold by a measure called the *board foot*. A board foot represents a piece of lumber 1 inch (or less) thick, 12 inches wide, and 1 foot long. Hardwood thicknesses are measured in quarter inches. The standard thicknesses are ¾, ⁴⁄₄, ⁵⁄₄, ⁶⁄₄, and ⁸⁄₄.

PLYWOOD

As you might guess, plywood is made from several plies of wood that are glued together. It is sold in sheets measuring 4 feet by 8 feet. In some supply stores you can also purchase half-sheets measuring 4 feet by 4 feet. Plywood comes in standard thicknesses of ⅛, ¼, ⅜, ½, ⅝, and ¾ inch.

There are two principal kinds of plywood: veneer-core and lumber-core. Lumber-core is the higher quality material; its edges can be worked as you would work solid wood. The exposed cut edges of veneer-core plywood must be either filled or covered because they are unsightly.

Plywood is also graded according to the quality of the outer veneer. The grades are A through D, with A representing the best quality. A piece of plywood has two designations, one for each face. For example, an A-D piece has one veneered surface that is A quality and one that is D quality.

Any outdoor project should be built using only exterior-rated plywood. This designation means that the glue between the plies is waterproof. Interior-grade plywood should not be used to construct outdoor pro-jects, as it will warp and split apart when exposed to the elements for even a very short period of time.

Paints and Stains

The finish that you apply to your completed project is extremely important when building anything that will be used outdoors. It goes without saying that you must choose an exterior-rated finish for any project that will be exposed to the elements. Your choice of finishes, and the care with which you apply it, will make a considerable difference in the look of your finished project. The better the finish, the longer you will be enjoying your handiwork.

There are hundreds of products on the market, but the first choice is whether to stain, paint, or simply seal your project. The advantages and disadvantages of each choice follow.

PAINT

Paint will cover a multitude of flaws. It is possible to take wood that is not at all attractive in appearance, apply a flawless coat of paint, and produce an extremely good-

Clockwise from bottom left: a natural-bristle brush; wood filler and putty knife; wood glue; an assortment of finishes, stains, paints, and sealant; and disposable foam brushes

looking piece of furniture. The disadvantage is that it must be thoroughly filled, sanded, and primed, all of which takes time and effort. Then it must be given two coats of paint, and at least one coat of sealer should be applied.

When shopping for paint, look for special characteristics that protect against local weather problems. For example, here in Florida, many paints are treated with special additives that protect against mildew, which occurs in our high humidity. Also look to see how long a warranty the paint has.

STAIN

Stains used to come in brown (or brown). True, there were gray-browns and yellow-browns and red-browns—but they were all brown nonetheless. And it used to be very difficult to apply them evenly. How times have changed! These days stains come in a terrific variety of colors—from the palest white to the darkest black. And they also range from extremely translucent to nearly opaque. They have an additional advantage of being extremely easy to apply and usually require only one coat.

Make certain that your stain is rated for exterior use. Although most manufacturers recommend that you apply their product with a brush, we have found that a plain old rag gives a very smooth and even appearance to most stains. (We do not guarantee best results with every type of stain, so we recommend you try it either on a scrap piece of wood or on a surface that will not show before attacking the entire project with our method.)

SEALER

The finish that will affect the wood's appearance the least is a clear wood finish, often referred to as a water sealer. It is most commonly used on decks and railings. Clear wood finish is available as an oil-based or as a waterborne product. Its actual appearance can range from a muted, almost invisible finish to a smooth, semigloss sheen. Make sure you buy a finish sealer, not a clear sanding sealer, which is used under paints and stains to prime the wood. You can apply a wood finish sealer with a brush or roller, or you can spray it on.

BRUSHES

Although most professionals swear by very expensive brushes, we use them only when there is absolutely no choice in the matter. We much prefer sponge brushes, which are extremely inexpensive and can be thrown in the trash after use. Look for the ones that have a smooth surface (like a cosmetic sponge) and a wooden handle. If you are interrupted in mid-coat, and the sponge brush is not yet ready for tossing, just pop your brush in an airtight sandwich bag. You can leave it there for a day or so, and it will remain pliable and ready to use.

TOOLS

From lower right: claw hammer, tack hammer and nail sets, and rubber mallet

If you are just beginning in woodworking, you may think you'll need to spend thousands of dollars on tools. Not true! Unless they are independently wealthy, most woodworkers start using hand tools and gradually add to their shop over time. Obviously, there were not many power tools when Louis XV's furniture craftsmen were at work—all of history's magnificent furniture was built using only hand tools.

The obvious reason for using power tools is that they get the job done faster. Our goal is to create a good-looking piece of furniture in the least amount of time. So over the years we have added power tools that cut the time required to complete the job and require a lot less physical effort. We use a power drill rather than a screwdriver and a circular saw rather than a hand saw. A good approach is to add a tool to your workshop each time you build a large project. You will still save a substantial amount of money (compared to purchasing the project in a store) and will then have the tool for the next project.

The projects in this book require some basic tools that, if you do not already own them, would make useful additions to any household. Some tools, such as a saw and a set of screwdrivers, are needed for every project, but others are required only for a few pieces. You may want to choose your first project according to the tools you have available. So it is a good idea to read through the instructions before starting a project, to determine which tools you will need. The tools required for the projects in this book make a good starting set of woodworking equipment.

If you are starting from scratch, buy the best tools you can afford. A bargain screwdriver that falls apart after inserting three screws is not much of a bargain, and the resulting frustration is not worth the two-dollar savings. Look for the manufacturer's warranty when purchasing tools. If they offer a lifetime guarantee, it's a safe bet that you'll be purchasing a good tool.

As with most hobbies, when you purchase your equipment, you should consider your physical size and ability. A golf club or a tennis racquet must be matched to the person using it. In the same way, a physically large person may be able to use a very large hammer. Although it is true that the larger hammer will drive the nail into the wood faster, it does not mean very much if you are able to swing a heavier hammer only twice before you feel your arm going weak from the strain. So try before you buy! Lift the tool a number of times before you purchase it. The same philosophy applies to power tools. It requires a great deal of strength to control a 4-inch-wide belt sander, but almost anyone can use a 2-inch-wide sander.

The following is our recommended list of tools to help you begin working with wood.

Basic Tools

Work surface that is smooth and level

Measuring tools: tape measure, level, and combination square

Hammers: two hammers (large and small), tack hammer, and nail set

Screwdrivers: an assortment of flathead and Phillips sizes

Saws: combination saw (or ripsaw and crosscut saw), circular saw, and a selection of blades

Drill: hand or power drill and a variety of bits

Clamps: Two "quick clamps" and two wood hand clamps

Sanding tools: sanding block and assortment of sandpaper (from fine to coarse)

Safety equipment: goggles and dust mask (use with power tools)

Optional Tools

Measuring tools: framing square

Clamps: two C clamps, a web clamp, and two bar clamps

Saws: saber saw, circular saw, and a selection of blades

Chisels: ¼-inch, ¾-inch, and 1-inch-wide

Finishing sander

Router

Advanced Tools

Belt sander

Table saw

Band saw

Drill press

Laser level

A hammer and saw probably come to mind when discussing woodworking. However, other tools are just as important. A solid work surface, a ready supply of clamps, and the right sanding equipment can make woodworking an enjoyable pursuit—and the lack of such tools can spell complete frustration.

Work Surface

Although most people would not put it at the top of the list, one of the most important tools in woodworking is a work surface that is smooth and level. If you construct a project on an uneven work surface, chances are that your table legs will be uneven or the cabinet top will slope downhill. Your work surface does not have to be a professional-quality mahogany workbench—it just has to be level and even. It can be as simple as an old door (flush, not paneled) or a piece of thick plywood supported by sawhorses.

To level your work surface, simply set a fairly long level in various places on the surface, turning it so that it faces in several directions. If necessary, shim the surface with thicknesses of wood to lift the surface enough to make it perfectly level. Be sure to attach the shim with glue and nails or screws to make certain that it stays in place while you work.

Clamps

Clamps are an absolute must for woodworking. They are used to apply pressure and hold joints together until the glue sets, and they are valuable aids when assembling a project. A single person can assemble a large project by using clamps—a job that otherwise requires the concerted effort of two or more people. When you buy clamps, it is advisable to get two clamps of the same type. This is because you almost always use them in pairs to provide even pressure on the work.

When you apply clamps, always insert a scrap piece of wood between the clamp and your work to act as a cushion. That way, you will avoid leaving clamp marks on the surface of your project.

There have been some fairly recent improvements in woodworking clamps. A new type looks like a regular bar clamp, but instead of a screw mechanism for tightening,

Battery-operated power drills (right), electric drill (lower left), and drill bits (upper left)

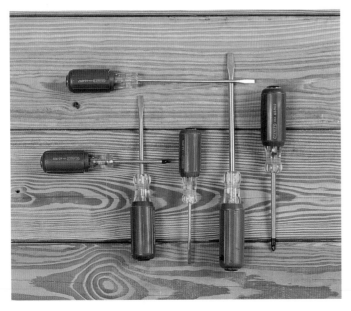

An assortment of screwdrivers

Clamps. Clockwise from upper right: C clamps (in two sizes), bar clamp, pipe clamp, hand clamp, web clamp, and spring clamp

ous lengths of pipe, depending upon the need. You can also buy rubber "shoes" that fit over the pipe clamp fittings, which will eliminate clamp marks on the wood.

Web clamps (or **band clamps**) are used for clamping such things as chairs or drawers, where a uniform pressure needs to be exerted completely around a project. It consists of a continuous band with an attached metal mechanism that can be ratcheted to pull the band tightly around the object.

Spring clamps are useful for quickly holding a piece of wood while you saw or for keeping two thin boards positioned. The 2-inch size is most useful because you can operate it with one hand.

Measuring Tools

If you have been involved with woodworking at all, you have probably heard the expression "measure twice, cut once." And it is always worth repeating. If you measure accurately and cut carefully to that measurement, your project will fit together perfectly during final assembly. And accurate cutting depends on accurate measurements. So a quality measuring tool is a sound investment. A wide steel tape rule is a good choice for most projects. A narrow tape will bend more easily along the length of a board and will be less accurate.

Consistently use the same measuring device throughout the cutting process. Unless you have precise measuring tools, any two instruments may vary enough to give you slightly different measurements.

If you are cutting a length of wood to fit between two existing pieces in an assembly, there is an even more accurate method of measurement than a steel tape. After you square off the wood you are cutting, simply hold it up to the actual space, and mark it for cutting.

A straightedge is a handy woodworking tool for quick measurements. An ordinary steel ruler, 12 to 24 inches long, is sufficient.

A sliding T-bevel is valuable for establishing bevel angles. The steel blade pivots and slides within a handle and can be locked in position to form an angle. It is used to check and transfer bevels and mitered ends.

Squares are versatile and essential tools in woodwork-

they have a trigger much like a caulk gun. This makes them especially useful, since they can be operated with one hand. They also have a quick-release mechanism. We recommend them for a beginner, since they are easy to use, work well, and come in a variety of lengths.

Old-fashioned **wood clamps** are a nice addition to your workshop. They are extremely versatile, since they can be adjusted to clamp offsetting surfaces.

C clamps are inexpensive and useful for many woodworking applications. One end of their C-shaped frame is fixed; the other end is fitted with a threaded rod and swivel pad that can be clamped tightly across an opening ranging from zero to several inches or more, depending on the size of the clamp. They can hold two thicknesses of wood together, secure a piece of wood to a work surface, and perform many other functions.

Bar clamps and **pipe clamps** can be used to hold assemblies together temporarily while fasteners are added, as well as to apply pressure to laminates. Although they look very much alike and function the same way, pipe clamps are significantly less expensive than bar clamps. You buy the fittings separately, and they can be used with vari-

Clockwise from top left: small (torpedo) level, chalk line, laser level, 4-foot level, 6-foot level, and combination laser level with attachment

ing. The most commonly used types are the framing square (or carpenter's square) and the combination square. In addition to their obvious use for marking a cutting line on a board and obtaining a right angle, squares can be used to check the outer or inner squareness of a joint, to guide a saw through a cut, and much more.

Cutting Tools

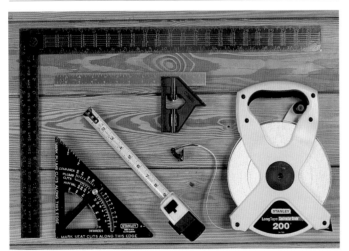

Measuring tools. Clockwise from top left: carpenter's square, combination square, open-reel long tape, tape measure, and combination speed square

Keep in mind that every saw blade has a thickness (called a *kerf*) that is removed from the wood when you cut. (From whence cometh the gigantic amount of sawdust that accumulates when you make a project.) When you measure and mark a board, measure precisely. When you cut the board at your mark, set the saw so that the blade will exactly remove the mark. Cut so that you also remove the mark from the end of the board that will be waste.

A piece of wood may be either *ripped* (cut along the length of the board) or *crosscut* (cut across the width of the board). There are specific hand tools for each procedure. A **rip saw** has teeth designed for cutting along the length of board, with the grain. It comes with 4½ through seven points per inch, the latter being the smoothest cut.

The **crosscut saw** is made to cut across the grain. Crosscut saws are available with seven through 12 points

Saws. Clockwise from top: back saw, crosscut saw (middle), miniature utility shortcut saw, tool-box saw (far right), finish saw (bottom), and saw-tooth set (below back saw)

per inch, depending on how coarse or fine you wish to the cut be. The greater the number, the smoother the cut.

Probably the most popular power cutting tool is the **circular saw**. The blade can be adjusted to cut at a 90° or

45° angle or any angle in between. Although **saw blades** for power tools are available for both ripping and crosscutting, the most practical blade for general woodworking is a combination blade. It rips and crosscuts with equal ease. Carbide-tipped blades are more expensive but well worth the cost, since they last much longer than regular blades.

The hand-held **jigsaw** or **saber saw** is used to cut curves, shapes, and large holes in panels or boards up to 1½ inches in thickness. Its cutting action comes from a narrow reciprocating îbayonetî blade that moves up and down very quickly. The best saber saws have a variable speed control and an orbital blade action, which swings the cutting edge forward into the work and back again during the blade's up-and-down cycle. A dust blower keeps the sawdust away from the cut.

A **power miter saw** is a favorite tool of ours. It can be used to efficiently cut boards to length and can be adjusted both horizontally from 90° to 1° and vertically from 45° to 1°. It is especially useful for cutting 45° miters.

When you are cutting either lumber or plywood, note the type of cut that your tool is making, and use it

to your advantage. For example, circular saws and saber saws cut on the upstroke, so they may leave ragged edges on the upper surface of your wood. When using these saws, you should position the wood with the better surface facing down.

Certain types of cuts, such as hollowing out a section of wood, are done with **chisels.** Using a chisel well takes some practice, but it is worth the effort because chisels can perform unique woodworking tasks. Always work with sharp chisels. For your first purchase, choose two different sizes—one very narrow and one about an inch wide.

If you need to shave just a small portion of wood off

An assortment of chisels (left) and scrapers (right)

the end or along the edge of a board, a plane is the appropriate tool. Again, buy a quality plane, and practice with it until you become fairly proficient.

Cutting Tools. Clockwise from right: jigsaw and jigsaw blades, circular saw, router and bits

An assortment of planes used to smooth wood surfaces

Sanding Tools. Clockwise from upper left: sheets of sandpaper, belt sander with belt, and orbital sander with sandpaper disks

Sanding Tools

Of course, any project may be sanded by hand. An inexpensive plastic sanding block will do the job of sanding a level surface just fine. You can even wrap a block of wood with a piece of sandpaper. If you need to sand moldings or curves, try wrapping a pencil or other appropriately sized object with sandpaper.

The amount of sanding that you do on each project depends, in large part, on the intended use of the project and on what kind of finish you plan to use. Obviously, if you prefer a rustic look for your project, it need not be sanded completely smooth. However, a rustic chair requires more sanding than a rustic table—someone will be sitting on it.

An **orbital sander** does a good job of beginning the sanding process, but it may leave circular marks that must be subsequently sanded out by hand.

A **finishing sander** is probably the most practical power sander for furniture projects. It has the ability to smooth the surface quickly, and it does not leave circular marks.

A **belt sander** is often used for large jobs. It sands quickly, but it is difficult to control on softwood such as pine. Because of its power, a belt sander can easily gouge

softwood, or if you do not watch carefully, it can remove more of the wood than you wish.

Files, which come in an assortment of shapes and sizes, are good tools for rough sanding work. No matter what tool you use, begin sanding with coarse grit and gradually progress to sandpaper with a fine grit.

An assortment of files for rough sanding work

Wood Joints

There are hundreds of different kinds of wood joints. They range in complexity from the plainest butt joint to incredibly intricate and time-consuming ones. The projects in this book are constructed with only the simplest joints, secured with glue and either nails or screws.

EDGE-TO-EDGE JOINT

This joint is used when laminating boards together edge to edge to obtain a wider piece of wood. To ensure a perfect meeting between boards, a minuscule amount should be ripped from the first side of each board. Then flip the board widthwise to rip the second edge to ensure complementary angles and a flat glued surface. Then apply glue to the adjoining edges and clamp the boards together.

Apply even pressure along the length of the piece. The boards should be firmly clamped, but not so tightly that all of the glue is forced out or that the lamination starts to bow across its width. On a long lamination, extra boards may be placed above and below the lamination, across the width, then clamped with C clamps or wood clamps. It is a good idea to put a piece of plastic or waxed paper between the piece and any wood clamped across the joints. This will eliminate the clamped board becoming a permanent part of the finished lamination. Wipe off any excess glue that is squeezed out in the clamping process.

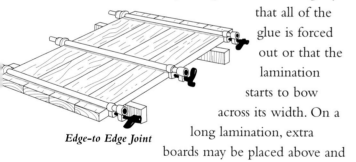

Edge-to Edge Joint

BUTT JOINT

This is the simplest of joints, where one board abuts another at a right angle. This method offers the least holding power of any joint. It must be reinforced with some kind of fastener, usually screws.

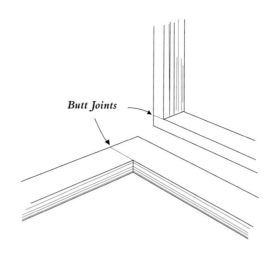

Butt Joints

MITER

A miter is a angle cut across the width of a board. It is used to joint two pieces of wood without exposing the end grain of either piece. A mitered joint must also be reinforced with nails or screws. The angle most often cut is 45°, which is used to construct a right angle when two mitered boards are joined together. The difference between a perfect miter and a none-too-perfect miter is the care in the measurement. When cutting and applying molding, begin at one end, cut the first piece, and attach it. Then cut the first angle on the second piece, hold it in place, and mark the cut (and the direction of that cut) on the other end. Since you are usually switching directions of 45° angles on each successive cut, this method avoids confusion. Attach the second piece, and continue the process for each subsequent piece. A helpful tip to make your miter joints look more perfect than they are is to firmly rub the length of the completed joint with the side of a pencil to smooth the two edges together.

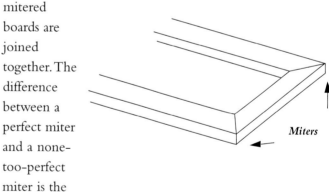

Miters

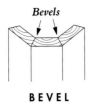

Bevels

BEVEL

A bevel is also an angular cut, but it refers to an angle cut along the length of a board, rather than across the width as in a miter.

DADO

A dado is a groove cut in the face of one board to accommodate the thickness of another board. It can be cut with a hand saw and chisel (see below, right), with a router, or with a dado set on a table saw.

No matter what kind of joint you are making, it is advisable to use both glue and fasteners (nails or screws) whenever possible. The only exception, when you may want to omit the glue, is on joints that you wish to disassemble at a later time.

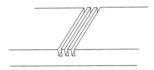

Cut dado to depth with saw.

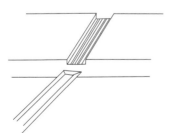

Use chisel to remove remaining wood from dado.

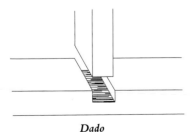

Dado

DRY-FITTING

Particularly if you are a beginner, you may wish to *dry-fit* your project. This means that you can preassemble portions of the project without glue to make certain that all of the pieces were cut correctly and fit together tightly. You can use clamps to hold the pieces together temporarily, or simply hammer small nails into the surface just far enough to hold them in place. Leave a large portion of the nail head above the surface, so the nails are easy to remove at a later date. Check the fit and trim or adjust the pieces as necessary. Then remove the clamps and/or nails, apply glue, and reassemble the pieces.

MEASURING LUMBER

Nothing is more frustrating than gathering the necessary materials and embarking upon a project only to find that inaccurate cutting has made it impossible for the pieces to fit together properly—and thus for the project to look right. Woodworking projects, regardless of the skill level, go much more smoothly if you follow the old adage "measure twice, cut once."

The best way to make good cuts is to measure accurately. There are a number of tools that will help with this: a wide steel tape rule, a square, and a variety of saws (see page 14 for more information on tools). It is essential that you buy or borrow quality tools. Whatever tools you choose, use the same measuring device throughout the project, as two instruments may vary enough to make a difference.

CUTTING LUMBER

The most important rule of thumb in cutting lumber is to cut the longest piece first. If you botch the cut, then you can still cut smaller pieces from the remaining board. It is also important to re-examine each piece of lumber one last time before you cut; this is useful in spotting end splits or knots that can be cut off.

If you plan carefully, you can cut so that all the best sides of the wood are facing out—this makes for the best possible use of your wood and saves you from having to fill and sand any imperfections after the project is finished.

Every time you use a blade to cut wood, the blade removes an amount of wood equal to the width of its saw blade, called the kerf. After you have precisely measured for a cut and marked it with a sharp pencil, set the saw so that the blade will exactly remove the waste side of the mark. Cut along the mark, trying to remove just half of your pencil line.

There are two types of cuts that can be made to a piece of wood: a rip or a crosscut. A rip is a cut along the length of the board, and a crosscut is a cut across the width of the board. There are specific hand tools for each procedure; see page 18 for detailed information on these cutting tools.

SAFETY

Working with power tools can be dangerous. In a battle with a power saw, you will be the loser. And losing is extremely painful. We know many woodworkers, and many of them have missing digits. If that sounds scary, thatís good. Read the instructions that are provided with every tool and follow them religiously. Again, we stress that these instructions are written for the beginner using hand tools; they must be altered when using power tools. Never attempt any woodworking maneuver that does not translate to power tools. Misuse of power tool equipment can lead to serious injury to yourself or damage to the tool.

Never take your eyes off the work; always concentrate on what you are doing, and take the necessary safety precautions. Just one moment of lost concentration or lack of adherence to safety rules can result in frightful consequences. Develop the habit of avoiding the path of the saw—do not stand directly behind it or directly in front of it. Power saws can flip a piece of wood back at you with incredible force.

Always wear safety goggles when working with wood. Avoiding just one splinter aimed at your eye makes this practice worth your while. A dust mask is a prudent accessory when working with wood. Sawdust can be very irritating to your lungs. You can choose from a number of

Clockwise from top: face shield, safety goggles, fire extinguisher, first-aid kit, paper dust mask, ear plugs, and dust mask with replaceable filters

different masks, from a simple paper mask to those with replaceable filters.

If you use power tools for extended periods—especially a power saw, which can be quite loud—a pair of ear plugs or protectors is a good investment. Prolonged exposure to loud noise can have harmful effects on your hearing.

Practicing all of these safety rules will keep you safe and make woodworking a pleasure.

Birdhouse Table

This whimsical table is one of our favorite projects, because it never fails to produce a smile on the faces of our backyard guests. Not only is it cheerful to behold, but the glass top makes it a practical addition to any outdoor room. We hope you will enjoy having one in your backyard.

Materials

4' x 4' sheet of ½" plywood	
7 linear feet of 1 x 1 pine	
4' x 4' sheet of ¼" plywood	
32 linear feet of ¾" screen molding	
4 linear feet of 1¼" L-shaped molding	
8 linear feet of 2 x 4 pine	
2 linear feet of 2 x 2 pine	
1 bundle of cedar shingles	

Hardware

70	1¼" (3d) finish nails
40	½" wire brads
200	1" wire brads
2	small drawer pulls
10	2½" (8d) finish nails
8	3" wood screws
4	corrugated metal fasteners

Special Tools and Techniques

Miter

Cutting List

Code	Description	Qty.	Materials	Dimensions
A	Front/Back	2	½" plywood	16" x 24"
B	Corner Supports	4	1 x 1 pine	17" long
C	Side	2	½" plywood	17" x 18"
D	Outer Roof	2	¼" plywood	10" x 23½"
E	Inner Roof	2	¼" plywood	8" x 23½"
F	Side Trim	4	¾" screen molding	16½" long
G	Center Trim	1	¾" screen molding	17" long
H	Outer Trim	4	¾" screen molding	18" long
I	Roof Trims	8	¾" screen molding	cut to fit
J	Peak Cover	2	1¼" L molding	23½" long
K	Doors	2	¼" plywood	8½" x 4½"
L	Horizontal Door Trim	4	¾" screen molding	3" long
M	Vertical Door Trim	4	¾" screen molding	8½" long
N	Window	4	¼" plywood	4½" x 4½"
O	Horizontal Window Trim	8	¾" screen molding	3" long
P	Vertical Window Trim	8	¾" screen molding	4½" long
Q	Long Base	2	2 x 4 pine	23½" long
R	Short Base	2	2 x 4 pine	21" long
S	Chimney	2	2 x 2 pine	10" long

Building the Basic House

1. Following the pattern in figure 1, cut two Front/Backs (A) from ½-inch plywood. Designate one as "Front" and one as "Back."

2. Drill four 1¼-inch-diameter holes in the Front (A), following the placement shown in figure 1. Do not drill any holes in the Back (A).

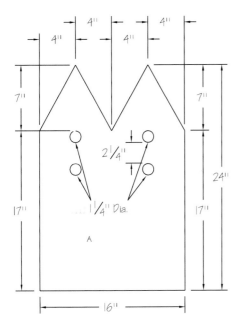

Figure 1

3. Cut four Corner Supports (B) from 1 x 1 pine, each measuring 17 inches.

4. Cut two Sides (C) from ½-inch plywood, each measuring 17 x 18 inches.

5. Position two Corner Supports (B) parallel to each other and 16½ inches apart. Place one Side (C) over the Corner Supports (B), matching the 17-inch edges, as shown in figure 2. Apply glue to the meeting surfaces, and nail through the Side (C) into the Corner Supports (B), using four evenly spaced 1¼-inch finish nails.

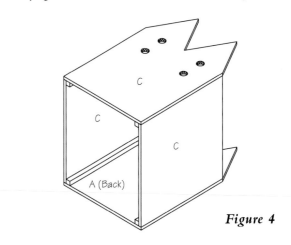

Figure 2

6. Repeat step 5 to attach the remaining two Corner Supports (B) to the remaining Side (C).

7. Place the Side (C) [with Corner Supports (B) on the top] on a level surface. Position the Front (A) perpendicular to the Side (C), matching the 17-inch edges, as shown in figure 3. Make certain that the outside edges are flush, then apply glue to the meeting surfaces, and nail through the Front (A) into the Corner Supports (B), using four evenly spaced 1¼-inch finish nails.

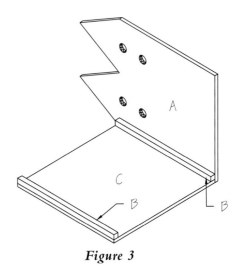

Figure 3

8. Repeat step 7 to attach the Back (A) to the opposite surface of the Side (C).

9. Position the remaining Side (C) over the assembly, aligning the 17-inch-long edges, as shown in figure 4. Apply glue to the meeting surfaces and nail through the Side (C) into the Corner Supports (B), using four evenly spaced 1¼-inch finish nails on each joint.

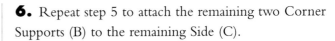

Figure 4

Adding the Roof

1. Cut two Outer Roofs (D) from ¼-inch plywood, each measuring 10 x 23½ inches.

2. Turn the assembly right side up, and fit one Outer Roof (D) over one top outer side of the assembly, over the edges of the Front (A), Back (A), and Side (C), as shown in figure 5. The Outer Roof (D) should be flush with the top

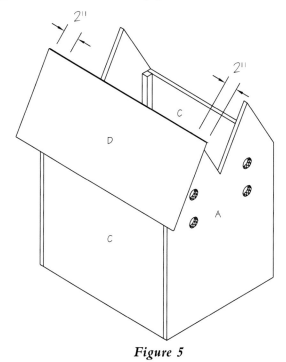

Figure 5

points of the Front and Back (A), and should extend 2 inches past the Front (A), Back (A), and Side (C), as shown in figure 5. Apply glue to the meeting surfaces, and nail through the Outer Roof (D) into the edges of the Front (A), Back (A), and Side (C), using 1-inch wire brads spaced about 2 inches apart.

3. Repeat step 2 to attach the remaining Outer Roof (D) to the opposite side of the house.

4. Cut two Inner Roofs (E) from ¼-inch plywood, each measuring 8 x 23½ inches.

5. Place one Inner Roof (E) over the edges of the Front (A) and Back (A). Check to make certain that the Inner Roof (E) does not overlap the edge of the Outer Roof

(D). Trim the width of the Inner Roof (E) if necessary. Apply glue to the meeting surfaces, and nail through the Inner Roof (E) into the Front (A) and Back (A), using four evenly spaced 1-inch wire brads on each joint.

6. Repeat step 5 to attach the remaining Inner Roof (E) to the opposite side of the assembly.

Adding the Trim

1. The next step is to add trim pieces to the front, corners, and roof of the birdhouse. If you wish to paint your birdhouse and do not plan to paint the trim, it is a good idea to do it now, before the trim pieces are added.

2. Cut four Side Trims (F) from ¾-inch-wide screen molding, each measuring 16½ inches.

3. Attach one Side Trim (F) flush with the bottom edge of the Side (C), over the joint between the Front (A) and Side (C). The Side Trims (F) are ½ inch shorter than the Sides (C) to accommodate the pitch of the roof. Apply glue to the meeting surfaces, and nail through the Side Trim (F) into the edge of the Front (A), using 1-inch wire brads spaced 2 inches apart.

4. Repeat step 3 three times to attach the remaining Side Trims (F) to the remaining joints between the Sides (C) and the Front (A) and Back (A).

5. Cut one Center Trim (G) from ¾-inch-wide screen molding, measuring 17 inches.

6. Place the Center Trim (G) on the Front (A), centered horizontally, as shown in figure 6 (see page 28). Apply glue to the meeting surfaces, and nail through the Center Trim (G) into the Front (A), using 1-inch wire brads spaced 2 inches apart.

7. Cut four Outer Trims (H) from ¾-inch-wide screen molding, each measuring 18 inches. Place one Outer Trim (H) over the joint between the Side Trim (H) and the Front (A). Mark the angle and cut the top end of the Outer Trim (H) to the proper angle. Apply glue to the

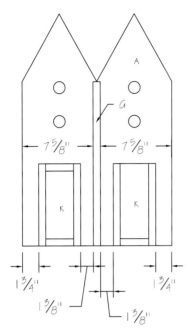

Figure 6

meeting surfaces, and nail through the Outer Trim (H) into the Front (A), using 1-inch wire brads spaced 2 inches apart.

8. Refer to the photograph for the placement of the Roof Trims (I); measure and cut eight Roof Trims (I) from ¾-inch-wide screen molding that fit over the exposed edges of the Outer and Inner Roofs (D and E), mitering them as shown in the photograph.

Adding the Shingles

1. We cut regular-size shingles into 6-inch lengths to match the reduced size of the birdhouse. It is better to work with the top portion of the original shingle, since that portion is thinner than the bottom edge. It is not difficult to shingle, and since the finished project should look somewhat rustic, the job is even easier.

2. Begin attaching the first row of shingles with 1-inch wire brads, just overlapping the bottom edge of one Outer Roof (D) with the first row of shingles. Each shingle should be nailed twice to prevent shifting. Shingles come in bundles containing random widths. Choose varying widths of shingles as you work across each row for a ran-

dom look. A row of narrow shingles followed by a row of wide shingles will look odd. Add a second row, overlapping the first row, about 3½ inches higher. Add a third row in the same manner. You may need to re-trim the length of the shingles on the third row, to make certain they don't extend past the roof's peak.

3. Repeat the application of shingles on the remaining Outer Roof (D).

4. Next, shingle the two Inner Roofs (E). These are shingled in the same manner, except that the Inner Roofs (E) are shorter, and therefore require only two rows of shingles. Try to match the rows of shingles on the Inner Roofs (E) to the rows on the Outer Roofs (D).

5. Cut two Peak Covers (J) from 1¼-inch L molding, each measuring 23½ inches.

6. Apply glue to the meeting surfaces, and nail the Peak Covers (J) over the shingles on the roof peak, using 1¼-inch finish nails spaced 2 inches apart.

Adding the Doors

1. Cut two Doors (K) from ¼-inch-thick plywood, each measuring 8½ x 4½ inches.

2. Cut four Horizontal Door Trims (L) from 3/4-inch-wide screen molding, each measuring 3 inches.

3. Cut four Vertical Door Trims (M) from ¾-inch-wide screen molding, each measuring 8½ inches.

4. Lay one Door (K) on a flat surface, then place two Vertical Door Trims (M) flush with the outer 8½-inch edge of the Door (K), as shown in figure 7. Apply glue to the meeting surfaces, and nail through the Vertical Door Trims (M) into the Door (K), using four ½-inch wire brads on each joint.

5. Place the two Horizontal Door Trims (L) between the two Vertical Door Trims (M), flush with the 4½-

Figure 7

inch edge of the Door (K). Apply glue to the meeting surfaces, and nail through the Horizontal Door Trims (L) into the Door (K), using two ½-inch wire brads on each joint.

6. Repeat steps 4 and 5 to assemble a second door.

7. Using figure 6 as a guide, attach the two completed doors to the Front (A). Apply glue to the meeting surfaces, and nail through the assembled door into the Front (A), using a 1-inch wire brad in each corner of the door.

8. Attach a small drawer pull to each of the doors for door handles.

Adding the Windows

1. Cut four Windows (N) from ¼-inch plywood, each measuring 4½ inches square.

2. Cut eight Horizontal Window Trims (O) from ¾-inch-wide screen molding, each measuring 3 inches.

3. Cut eight Vertical Window Trims (P) from ¾-inch-wide screen molding, each measuring 4½ inches.

4. Lay one Window (N) on a flat surface, and position two Vertical Window Trims (P) flush with the outer edges of the Window (N), in the same manner as for the door trims. Apply glue to the meeting surfaces, and nail through the Vertical Window Trims (P) into the Window (N), using four ½-inch wire brads on each joint.

5. Position the two Horizontal Window Trims (O) between the two Vertical Window Trims (P), flush with the edges of the Window (N). Apply glue to the meeting surfaces, and nail through the Horizontal Window Trims (O) into the Window (N), using two ½-inch wire brads on each joint.

6. Repeat steps 4 and 5 three times to assemble three additional windows.

7. Using figure 8 as a placement guide, attach two windows to each Side (C). Apply glue to the meeting surfaces, and nail through the completed window into the Side (C), using one 1-inch wire brad on each corner of the window.

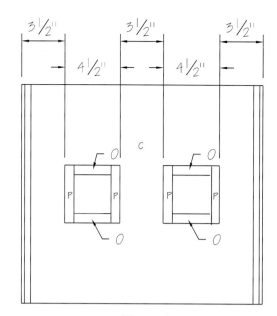

Figure 8

Adding the Base

1. Cut two Long Bases (Q) from 2 x 4 pine, each measuring 23-½ inches.

2. Cut two Short Bases (R) from 2 x 4 pine, each measuring 21 inches.

3. Miter the ends of the Long and Short Bases (Q and R) at opposing 45° angles, as shown in figure 9.

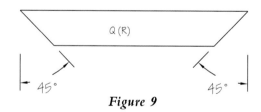

Figure 9

4. Position the two Long Bases (Q) on a flat surface, parallel to each other and 14 inches apart. Fit the two Short Bases (R) at the ends of the two Long Bases (Q) to form a 23½- x 21-inch rectangle, as shown in figure 10 (see page 30). Apply glue to the meeting surfaces, and screw through both sides of each corner, using two 3-inch screws on each corner. Reinforce each joint by adding a corrugated metal fastener across the inner corner of each joint.

5. Center the assembled birdhouse table over the base, making certain that the base extension is the same on all

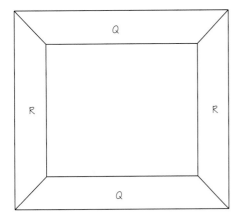

Figure 10

four sides. Toenail through the lower edges of the Front (A), Back (A), and Sides (C) into the base, using 2½-inch finish nails spaced about every 2 inches around the perimeter.

6. An optional step at this point is to measure and miter ¾-inch-wide screen molding around the vertical trims at all four corners.

Adding the Chimneys

1. To help support the glass tabletop, we added two chimneys to the birdhouse. Cut two Chimneys (S) from 2 x 2 pine, each measuring 10 inches.

2. Hold the Chimney (S) so that one end is level with the top of the birdhouse roofs, and mark the roof angle on the Chimney (S), so that the top of the Chimney (S) will sit level with the peak of the roof. Use the mark to trim the Chimney (S).

3. Repeat step 2 to trim the remaining Chimney (S).

4. Apply glue to the meeting surfaces, and attach both Chimneys (S) to the roof, halfway between the front and back of the birdhouse. Nail through the lower ends of the Chimney (S) into the shingled roof, using two 2½-inch finish nails on each Chimney (S).

Finishing

1. Fill any cracks, crevices, and nail holes with wood filler.

2. Sand the wood filler and any other unsanded surfaces.

3. Paint or stain the remaining portions of the birdhouse table, or simply seal it with a clear varnish.

4. Place the circular glass tabletop on the completed birdhouse base.

No matter where you live, it seems outdoor privacy is always needed. This screen is portable enough to be moved occasionally but sturdy enough to avoid blowing over. Use it to define an outdoor living space or to screen out an undesirable view.

Materials

65 linear feet of 2 x 4 pine

120 linear feet of 1 x 1 pine

4' x 8' sheet of privacy lattice

Hardware

35 3" wood screws

350 1¼" (3d) finish nails

9 3" hinges

Cutting List

Code	Description	Qty.	Materials	Dimensions
A	Long Side	8	2 x 4 pine	75" long
B	Short Side	8	2 x 4 pine	12" long
C	Long Trim	16	1 x 1 pine	72" long
D	Short Trim	16	1 x 1 pine	10½" long
E	Lattice Inserts	4	Privacy lattice	12" x 72"

Building the Frames

1. Cut eight Long Sides (A) from 2 x 4 pine, each measuring 75 inches.

2. Cut eight Short Sides (B) from 2 x 4 pine, each measuring 12 inches.

3. Position two of the Short Sides (B) on edge, parallel to each other and 72 inches apart. Place the Long Sides (A) over the ends of the Short Sides (B), as shown in figure 1. Apply glue to the meeting surfaces, and screw through the Long Sides (A) into the ends of the Short Sides (B), using two 3-inch wood screws on each joint.

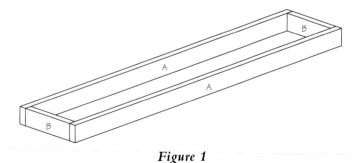

Figure 1

4. Repeat step 3 to build three more frames.

Adding the Lattice

1. Cut 16 Long Trims (C) from 1 x 1 pine, each measuring 72 inches.

2. Cut 16 Short Trims (D) from 1 x 1 pine, each measuring 10½ inches.

3. Attach one of the Long Trims (C) to the inside of one Long Side (A) ¾ inch from the edge, as shown in figure 2. Apply glue to the meeting surfaces, nail through the Long

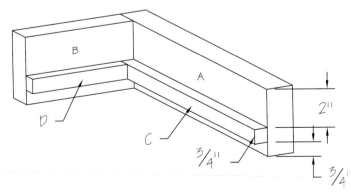

Figure 2

Trims (C) into the face of the Long Side (A), using 1¼-inch finish nails spaced every 4 inches.

4. Repeat step 3 for the remaining Long Sides (A).

5. Attach one of the Short Trims (D) to the inside of the Short Side (B), again ¾ inch in from the edge. Apply glue to the meeting surfaces, and nail through the Short Trim into the face of the Short Side (B), using 1¼-inch finish nails spaced every 4 inches.

6. Repeat step 5 for the remaining Short Sides (B).

7. Cut four Lattice Inserts (E) from a 4- x 8-foot sheet of privacy lattice, each measuring 12 x 72 inches.

8. Place the Lattice Inserts (E) inside the assembled frames, on top of the Long and Short Trims (C and D), as shown in figure 3.

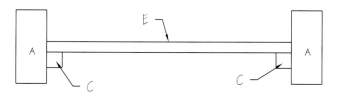

Figure 3

9. Repeat steps 3 through 5 to add two Short Trims (D) and two Long Trims (C) on the opposite side of the lattice insert (E), as shown in figure 4, then assemble three more identical screen sections.

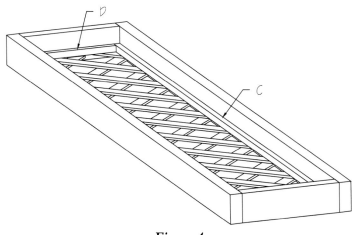

Figure 4

Finishing

1. We used three hinges between each of the main panels. Remember when attaching the hinges to alternate them so the screen will fold properly. The hinge peg faces the back of the screen between the two middle panels and faces the front of the screen on the outer panels.

2. Fill any screw or nail holes with wood filler.

3. Sand screen thoroughly.

4. Paint or stain the screen the color of your choice, or leave natural.

Lawn Chair

These simple-to-make chairs are a great addition to any backyard or deck—and even without a pillow, they are surprisingly comfortable. A great way to add seating to your backyard living space when you have very little time and money.

Materials

17 linear feet of 2 x 4 pine

30 linear feet of 1 x 4 pine

Hardware

95   2½" wood screws

4   3½" carriage bolts

4   3½" lag screws

Special Tools and Techniques

Bar clamps

Cutting List

Code	Description	Qty.	Materials	Dimensions
A	Seat Front	1	2 x 4 pine	20" long
B	Seat Side	2	2 x 4 pine	19" long
C	Seat Slat	5	1 x 4 pine	20" long
D	Back Support	2	2 x 4 pine	14½" long
E	Back	5	1 x 4 pine	20" long
F	Arm	2	1 x 4 pine	21" long
G	Arm Support	4	2 x 4 pine	24" long

Building the Seat

1. Cut one Seat Front (A) from 1 x 4 pine, measuring 20 inches.

2. Cut two Seat Sides (B) from 2 x 4 pine, each measuring 19 inches.

3. Position the two Seat Sides (B) on edge, parallel to each other and 17 inches apart. Fit the Seat Front (A) over the ends of the Seat Sides (B), as shown in figure 1. Apply glue to the meeting surfaces, and screw through the Seat Front (A) into the ends of the Seat Sides (B), using two 2½-inch wood screws on each joint.

4. Cut five Seat Slats (C) from 1 x 4 pine, each measuring 20 inches.

5. Place the seat assembly [Seat Front (A) and Seat Sides (B)] on a flat surface. Position the five Seat Slats (C) over the assembly, as shown in figure 2. The first Seat Slat (C) should be set back ½ inch from the face of the Seat Front (A), and the Seat Sides (B) should remain exposed at the other end. Screw through the Seat Slats (C) into the Seat Sides (B), using two 2½-inch wood screws on each joint.

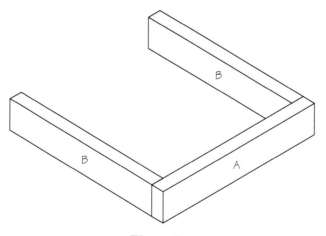

Figure 1

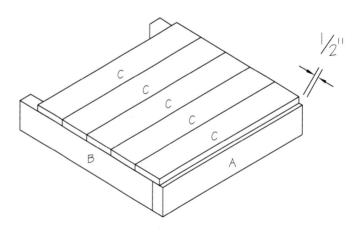

Figure 2

Making the Back

1. Cut two Back Supports (D) from 2 x 4 pine, each measuring 14½ inches.

2. Cut five Backs (E) from 1 x 4 pine, each measuring 20 inches.

3. Position the two Back Supports (D) on a flat surface, parallel to each other and 13 inches apart. Position one Back (E) over the two Back Supports (D), as shown in figure 3. The first Back (E) should overhang the ends of the two Back Supports (D) by 1 inch. Apply glue to the meeting surfaces, and screw through the Back (E) into each of the Back Supports (D), using two 2½-inch wood screws on each joint.

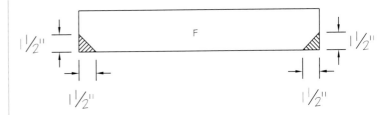

Figure 4

3. Cut four Arm Supports (G) from 2 x 4 pine, each measuring 24 inches.

4. Position two Arm Supports (G) face down on a level surface, parallel to each other and 12 inches apart. Place one Arm (F), uncut edge down, over the ends of the two Arm Supports (G), as shown in figure 5. The Arm (F) should overlap each of the Arm Supports (G) by 1 inch on each side. Apply glue to the meeting surfaces, and screw through the Arm (F) into the end of the Arm Supports (G), using two 2½-inch wood screws on each joint.

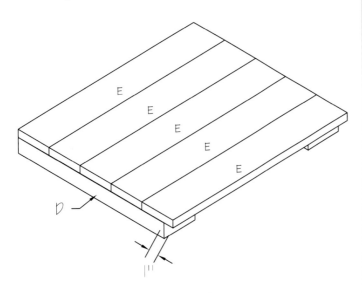

Figure 3

4. Repeat step 3 four times to attach the remaining four Backs (E) to the two Back Supports (D).

Making the Sides

1. Cut two Arms (F) from 1 x 4 pine, each measuring 21 inches.

2. Using figure 4 as a guide, shape the one Arm (F) by eliminating cutting off the shaded portions. Use the shaped Arm (F) as a pattern to cut the remaining Arm (F).

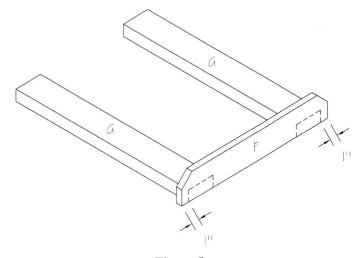

Figure 5

5. Repeat step 4 to construct another side, using the remaining two Arm Supports (G) and the remaining Arm (F).

Attaching the Arms

1. Draw a line across the inside of each Arm Support (G), 18 inches from the unattached end. This will be the placement line for the next step.

2. This step is easier with a helper. The object is to clamp the assembled seat between the two side assemblies (as shown in figure 6), then secure the seat with carriage bolts. The top of the seat should be positioned at the placement marks that you drew on the Arm Supports (G). The front Arm Supports (G) should be positioned 2 inches from the front of the seat assembly. When the sides are in position, clamp the two sides and seat assemblies tightly together, using bar clamps.

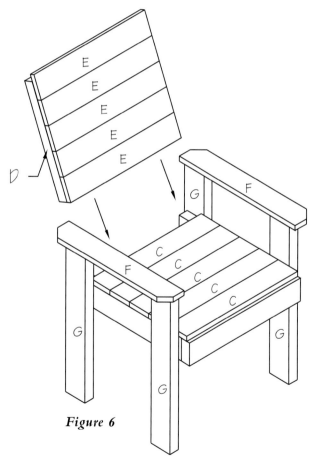

Figure 6

3. Drill a hole slightly larger than the diameter of the 3½-inch carriage bolt through the center of each of the Arm Supports (G) and into the Seat Sides (B). Then insert a 3½-inch carriage bolt through each of the holes. Tighten the bolts securely.

Adding the Back

1. Insert the back assembly between the two assembled sides. The Backs (E) should face the front of the chair, and the recessed end of the two Back Supports (D) should be at the top of the chair. To make the chair more comfortable, tilt the back assembly at a slight angle—out at the top and in at the bottom. The tilt angle is determined by the width of the 2 x 4 on the Arm Supports (G) and the back of the Arm (F).

2. When you have the back fitted perfectly, secure the assembly with bar clamps. Screw through the Arm Supports (H) into the Back Supports (E), using two 2½-inch wood screws. Then insert a 3½-inch lag screw through the Arm Supports (H) and into the Back Supports (E).

Finishing

1. Fill any cracks, crevices, or screw holes with wood filler.

2. Sand the completed chair thoroughly.

3. Paint or stain the chair the color of your choice—or simply leave it the natural color.

When you entertain outside, where do you put all the crummy-looking supplies that you use to maintain your outdoor room? Here's a simple solution: Store them behind the door of this great-looking storage shed. Your supplies will be out of sight, but close at hand.

Materials

12 linear feet of 2 x 4 pine

4' x 8' sheet of ½" exterior grooved plywood paneling

4' x 4' sheet of ½" exterior plywood

½ bundle of cedar shingles

3 linear feet of 1½"-wide lath

7 linear feet of 2 x 2 pine

Hardware

20 3½" wood screws

150 1¼" (3d) finish nails

100 1" wire brads

20 2" (6d) finish nails

3 exterior hinges

1 exterior door latch

Special Tools and Techniques

Sabre saw

Cutting List

Code	Description	Qty.	Materials	Dimensions
A	Long Inner Supports	4	2 x 4 pine	22½" long
B	Short Inner Supports	4	2 x 4 pine	8½" long
C	Front/Back	2	½" paneling	23½" x 80"
D	Side	2	½" paneling	11½" x 72"
E	Roof	2	½" plywood	13½" x 17"
F	Roof Trim	2	1½" lath	17" long
G	Shelf	4	½" plywood	11½" x 22½"
H	Shelf Support	9	2 x 2 pine	8½" long

Building the Frame

1. Cut four Long Inner Supports (A) from 2 x 4 pine, each measuring 22½ inches.

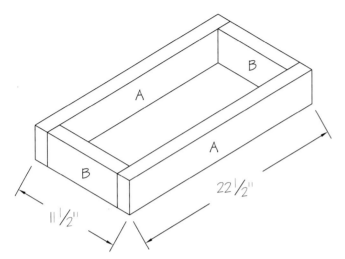

Figure 1

2. Cut four Short Inner Supports (B) from 2 x 4 pine, each measuring 8½ inches.

3. Position two of the Short Inner Supports (B) on edge, parallel to each other and 19½ inches apart. Place two of the Long Inner Supports (A) over the ends of the Short Inner Supports (B) to form a rectangle measuring 22½ x 11½ inches. Apply glue to the meeting surfaces, and screw through the Long Inner Supports (A) into the ends of the Short Inner Supports (B), using two 3½-inch wood screws on each joint. See figure 1.

4. Repeat step 3 to assemble a second rectangle. Designate one rectangle as "Top" and one as "Bottom."

5. Cut two Front/Backs (C) from ½-inch-thick exterior grooved plywood, each measuring 23½ x 80 inches. Because you will use the grooves in the paneling as guides to create the door, place one of the paneling grooves down the exact vertical center of one Front/Back (C), and label that piece "Front."

6. Using figure 2 as a guide, cut the door portion out of the Front (C). Since our plywood paneling was grooved every 3½ inches, we simply used the grooves as a guide to

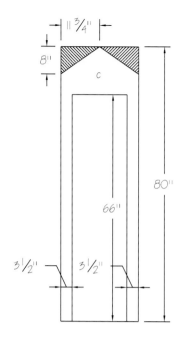

Figure 2

cut the door. Mark the cutting lines, and use a sabre saw to cut vertically up one groove, across the top, and down the groove on the opposite side.

7. Using figure 2 as a guide, trim off the top two corners of the Front/Backs (A), eliminating the shaded portions.

8. Cut two Sides (D) from ½-inch-thick grooved plywood, each measuring 11½ x 72 inches.

9. Position the two assembled Top and Bottom rectangles, parallel to each other and 64 inches apart, placing the Long Inner Supports (A) against the work surface. Place the Sides (D) against the Short Inner Supports (B), as shown in figure 3. Apply glue to the meeting surfaces, and nail through the Sides (D) into the Short Inner Supports (B), using 1¼-inch finish nails about every 4 inches.

10. Place the Front (C) against the Long Inner Supports (A), as shown in figure 4. Apply glue to the meeting surfaces, and nail through the Front (C) into the Long Inner Supports (A), using 1¼-inch finish nails spaced every 4 inches.

11. Turn the assembly over, and repeat step 10 to attach the Back (C) to the assembly, using the same procedure you used to attach the Front (C).

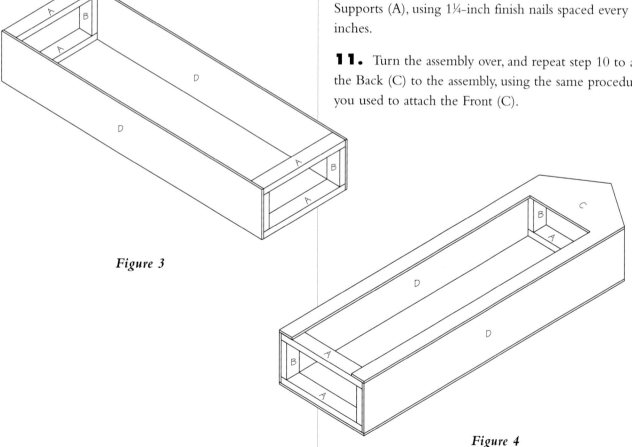

Figure 3

Figure 4

Adding the Roof

1. Cut two Roofs (E) from ½-inch plywood, each measuring 13½ x 17 inches.

2. Position the two Roofs (E) over the top of the assembly, so that they meet at the peak, as shown in figure 5. Note that the Roofs (E) are flush with the Back (C) and overhang the Front (C). Do not worry about the resulting gap at the roof peak; it will be covered with shingles in the next step. Apply glue to the meeting surfaces, and nail through the Roofs (E) into the edges of the Front (C), Back (C), and Sides (D), using 1¼-inch finish nails spaced about every 3 inches.

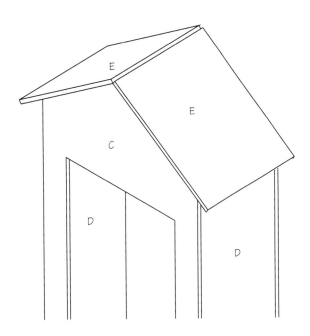

Figure 5

Adding the Shingles

1. Use three rows of shingles to cover each side of the roof of the storage center. On the second and third rows, trim regular-size shingles to the appropriate length, so they do not extend past the roof peak. It is better to work with the top portion of the original shingle, since it is thinner than the bottom edge. It is not difficult to shingle, and since the finished project should look somewhat rustic, this job is even easier. Begin attaching the first row of shingles with 1-inch wire brads, just overlapping the bottom edge of one Roof (D). Each shingle should be nailed twice to prevent shifting. Choose varying widths of shingles as you work. Continue the row across the bottom edge.

2. Next, add a second row overlapping the first row, about 6 inches higher. Then add a third row, overlapping the second row, again about 6 inches higher.

3. Repeat the application of shingles on the remaining Roof (D). Try to match the rows of shingles on the two Roofs (D).

4. To cover the roof peak, cut the shingles to 1½ inches wide, and attach the resulting narrow shingles to both sides of the peak, working from the front to the back of the roof. Add three rows, trimming the shingles to length so they do not extend past the back edges of the roof.

Adding the Roof Trims

1. Cut two Roof Trims (F) from 1½-inch-wide lath, each measuring 17 inches.

2. Refer to the photograph on page 43 of the finished project to miter the ends of the trim to cover the front exposed edges of the Roofs (E). Apply glue to the meeting surfaces, and nail through the Roof Trims (F) into the edge of the Roofs (E), using 1-inch wire brads spaced about 2 inches apart.

Adding the Shelves

1. Cut four Shelves (G) from ½-inch plywood, each measuring 11½ x 22½ inches.

2. Fit one Shelf (G) over the Bottom rectangle inside the storage center. Apply glue to the meeting surfaces, and nail through the Shelf (G) into the Long and Short Inner Supports (A and B), using 1¼-inch finish nails spaced every 4 inches.

3. Cut nine Shelf Supports (H), each measuring 8½ inches. These will be attached to the Sides (D), Front (C), and Back (C) to support the three upper shelves. The exact positioning of the three additional shelves is a matter of personal preference. We installed the lower of these shelves 12 inches above the bottom shelf, the next one 12 inches above that shelf, and the top shelf 18 inches above the middle shelf.

4. When you have decided on the placement of the shelves, mark the position of each shelf on the Back (C) and the Sides (D). Next, install three Shelf Supports (H) for each shelf: one in the center of the Back (C) and one in the center of each Side (D). Make certain that the Shelf Supports (H) are perfectly level, or your contents will end up in a heap on one side of the shelf. Apply glue to the meeting surfaces, and nail through the Shelf Support (H) into the Back (C) or Side (D), using two 2-inch finish nails on each Shelf Support (H). Do not countersink the nail, or it will show up on the outside of the storage center.

5. Install the Shelves (G) on top of the Shelf Supports (H).

Finishing

1. Install the door, using three exterior hinges.

2. Install the door latch.

3. Very little sanding is required on this project, as the paneling is supposed to keep its rustic look. Simply remove any obvious splinters or rough edges.

4. You can either paint or stain the storage center the color of your choice, or leave it natural. Here, the storage center has been painted light blue and the roof painted black.

Tuteur

M odeled after the vine trellises in Europe, this tuteur not only looks great, but provides a place for vines to grow and be protected. The unique shape will add interest to your garden, without taking up much space.

Materials

50 linear feet of 1 x 4 pine

23 linear feet of 1 x 1 pine

10" x 10" square of ¾" exterior plywood

Fence-post finial

Hardware

50 1¼" wood screws

30 1¼" (3d) finish nails

50 1⅝" wood screws

Special Tools and Techniques

Miter

Cutting List

Code	Description	Qty.	Materials	Dimensions
A	Vertical	8	1 x 4 pine	51" long
B	Center Vertical	4	1 x 1 pine	51" long
C	Short Top Support	2	1 x 4 pine	7¾" long
D	Short Middle Support	2	1 x 4 pine	11¼" long
E	Short Bottom Support	2	1 x 4 pine	13½" long
F	Long Top Support	2	1 x 4 pine	9¼" long
G	Long Middle Support	2	1 x 4 pine	12¾" long
H	Long Bottom Support	2	1 x 4 pine	15" long
I	Top	1	¾" plywood	10½" square
J	Top Trim	4	1 x 1 pine	12" long

Cutting the Wide Side Pieces

1. Cut eight Verticals (A) from 1 x 4 pine, each measuring 51 inches.

2. Miter each end of each Vertical (A) at a 5° angle, as shown in figure 1.

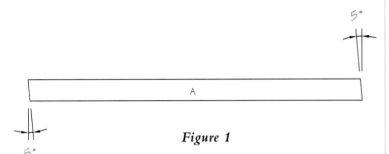

Figure 1

3. Cut four Center Verticals (B) from 1 x 1 pine, each measuring 51 inches.

4. Cut two Short Top Supports (C) from 1 x 4 pine, each measuring 7¾ inches.

5. Miter each of the Short Top Supports (C) at opposing 5° angles, as shown in figure 2.

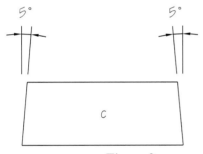

Figure 2

6. Cut two Short Middle Supports (D) from 1 x 4 pine, each measuring 11¼ inches.

7. Miter the ends of each of the two Short Middle Supports (D) at opposing 5° angles, as shown in figure 2.

8. Cut two Short Bottom Supports (E) from 1 x 4 pine, each measuring 13½ inches.

9. Miter the ends of each of the two Short Bottom Supports (E) at opposing 5° angles, as shown in figure 2.

Assembling the Wide Sides

1. Position two Verticals (A) on a level work surface so that they form an upside-down V-shape that is open at the top (see figure 3). The Verticals (A) should be 8⅝ inches apart at the top, and 17½ inches apart at the bottom.

2. The sides of the finished tuteur should slope in at the top and out at the bottom. Each of the sides has three horizontal supports that determine the angle of the slope. Place all of the Supports (C, D, and E) on the Verticals (A) to make certain that the side is properly assembled before attaching any of the supports to the Verticals (A). Refer to figure 3 to check your measurements.

3. Position one Short Top Support (C) on top of the two Verticals (A), flush with the top of the assembly. Position one Short Bottom Support (E) over the two Verticals (A), flush with the bottom of the assembly. Position one Short Middle Support (D) over the Verticals (A) in the middle of the assembly, as shown in figure 3. Once all the supports are positioned correctly, apply glue to the meeting surfaces, and screw through the Short Top, Middle, and Bottom Supports (C, D, and E) into the Verticals (A), using two 1¼-inch wood screws on each joint.

4. Turn the side assembly upside down, so that the Verticals (A) are on the top. Place one Center Vertical (B) between the two Verticals (A), on top of the Short Top, Middle, and Bottom Supports (C, D, and E), as shown in figure 4. Apply glue to the meeting surfaces, and nail through the Center Vertical (B) into the Short Top, Middle, and Bottom Supports (C, D, and E), using a 1¼-inch finish nail on each joint.

5. Repeat steps 1 through 4 to form a second wide side. There should be four Verticals (A) and two Center Verticals (B) remaining. Set them aside for use in the next assemblies.

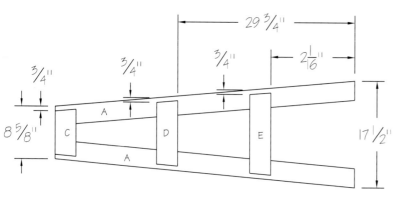

Figure 3

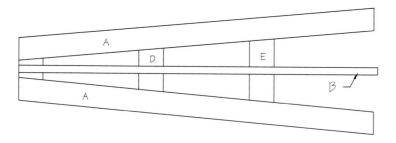

Figure 4

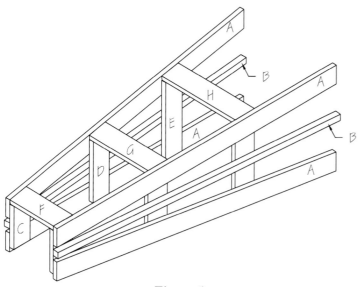

Figure 5

Cutting the Narrow Sides

1. Cut two Long Top Supports (F) from 1 x 4 pine, each measuring 9¼ inches.

2. Miter each of the Long Top Supports (F) at opposing 5° angles, as shown in figure 2.

3. Cut two Long Middle Supports (G) from 1 x 4 pine, each measuring 11¼ inches.

4. Miter the ends of each of the two Long Middle Supports (G) at opposing 5° angles, as shown in figure 2.

5. Cut two Long Bottom Supports (H) from 1 x 4 pine, each measuring 15 inches.

6. Miter the ends of each of the two Long Bottom Supports (H) at opposing 5° angles, as shown in figure 2.

Connecting the Frame

1. Position the two vertical assemblies (pieces A through E) opposite each other, as shown in figure 5.

2. Place one Long Top Support (F) over the ends of the Short Top Supports (C), as shown in figure 5. Apply glue to the meeting surfaces, and screw through the Long Top Support (F) into the end of the Short Top Supports (C), using 1¼-inch wood screws spaced about 6 inches apart.

3. Repeat step 2 to attach the remaining Long Middle and Top Supports (G and H), as shown in figure 5.

4. Turn the assembly over and repeat steps 2 and 3 to attach the remaining Long Top, Middle, and Bottom Supports (F, G, and H).

5. Place one Vertical (A) against the edge of another Vertical (A) and Long Top, Middle, and Bottom Supports (F, G, and H), as shown in figure 6 (see page 48). Apply glue to the meeting surfaces, and screw through the Vertical (A) into the Long Top, Middle, and Bottom Supports (F, G, and H) and into the Vertical (A), using two 1¼-inch wood screws in each joint spaced every 6 inches along the Vertical (A).

6. Repeat step 5 to attach another Vertical (A).

7. Turn the assembly over and repeat steps 5 and 6 to attach the remaining two Verticals (A).

8. Position one Center Vertical (B) between the two Verticals (A), over the Long Top, Middle, and Bottom Supports (F, G, and H), as shown in figure 6. Apply glue to the meeting surfaces, and nail through the Center Vertical (B) into the Long Top, Middle, and Bottom Supports (F, G, and H), using a 1¼-inch finish nail on each joint.

9. Repeat step 8 for the remaining Center Vertical (B).

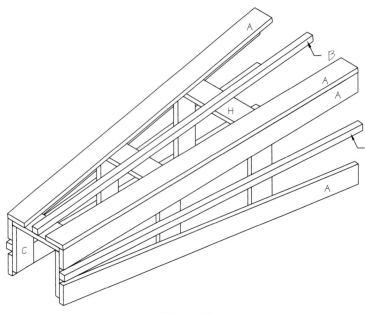

Figure 6

Finishing

1. Cut one Top (I) from ¾-inch-thick plywood, measuring 10½ inches square.

2. Stand the tuteur upright, and center the Top (I) over the ends of the Verticals (A). Apply glue to the meeting surfaces, and screw through the Top (I) into the Verticals (A), using two 1⅝-inch wood screws on each side.

3. Locate and mark the center of the Top (I). Predrill a starter hole, then screw the fence-post finial to the Top (I).

4. Cut four Top Trims (J) from 1 x 1 pine, each measuring 12 inches.

5. Miter the ends of each of the Top Trims (J) at opposing 45° angles.

6. Working around the Top (I) in rotation, glue and nail each of the Top Trims (J) over the edges of the Top (I), matching miters on all four corners. Use three 1¼-inch finish nails on each Top Trim (J). (See figure 7.)

7. Stain or paint the finished tuteur the color of your choice, or simply leave it natural.

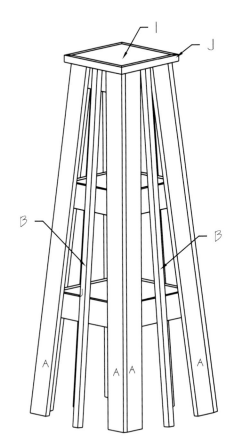

Figure 7

Porch Swing

Once a favorite of my grandmother's, this wonderful seat is now a favorite of ours. In fact, this wooden porch swing is just like the one my grandmother had on her front porch. It is a peaceful place for resting, and brings back memories of the neighbors coming to call.

Materials

20 linear feet of 2 x 4 pine

30 linear feet of ¾ pine decking

5 linear feet of 1 x 4 pine

Hardware

35 2½" wood screws

12 2" wood screws

4 3½" lag screws

4 3½" lag bolts

4 3" eye bolts

Chain and fittings for hanging swing*

*Notes on Materials

Because each situation is unique, we have not specified the hardware necessary to hang the swing, though it is very important to make certain that the swing is hung securely. We suggest that it be hung only from an extremely solid structural member on your porch or deck. We used chain and eye bolts rated to hold 1,500 pounds. We do not really expect it to have to bear that kind of weight, but it is better to be safe than sorry. If you are in doubt about your particular situation, consult an expert at your local hardware or building supply store.

Special Tools and Techniques

Bar clamps

Cutting List

Code	Description	Qty.	Materials	Dimensions
A	Seat Front/Back	2	2 x 4 pine	48" long
B	Seat Side	2	2 x 4 pine	19" long
C	Seat Support	1	2 x 4 pine	19" long
D	Seat Slat	4	¾ pine decking	48" long
E	Back Support	2	2 x 4 pine	16" long
F	Back	3	¾ pine decking	48" long
G	Arm	2	1 x 4	26" long
H	Arm Support	4	2 x 4	11½" long

Building the Seat

1. Cut two Seat Front/Backs (A) from 2 x 4 pine, each measuring 48 inches.

2. Cut two Seat Sides (B) from 2 x 4 pine, each measuring 19 inches.

3. Place the two Seat Front/Backs (A) on edge, parallel to each other and 19 inches apart. Fit the two Seat Sides (B) between the ends of the Seat Front/Backs (A) to form a rectangle measuring 22 x 48 inches, as shown in figure 1. Apply glue to the meeting surfaces, and screw through the Seat Front/Backs (A) into the ends of the Seat Sides (B), using two 2½-inch wood screws on each joint.

4. Cut one Seat Support (C) from 2 x 4 pine, measuring 19 inches.

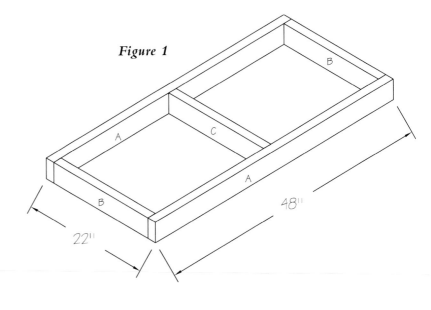

Figure 1

5. Place the Seat Support (C) in the center of the rectangle, parallel to and centered between the two Seat Sides (B), as shown in figure 1 (page 52).

6. Cut four Seat Slats (D) from ¾ pine decking, each measuring 48 inches.

7. Place the rectangular seat assembly (Seat Front/Backs [A], two Seat Sides [B], and Seat Support [C]) on a flat surface. Position the four Seat Slats (D) over the assembly, as shown in figure 2. Screw through the Seat Slats (D) into the Seat Sides (B) and Seat Support (C), using two 2½-inch wood screws on each joint.

Making the Back

1. Cut two Back Supports (E) from 2 x 4 pine, each measuring 16 inches

2. Cut three Backs (F) from ¾ pine decking, each measuring 48 inches.

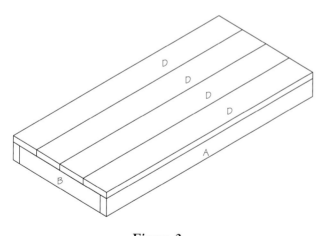

Figure 2

3. Position the two Back Supports (E) on a flat surface, parallel to each other and 41 inches apart. Place one Back (F) over the two Back Supports (E), as shown in figure 3.

4. The first Back (F) should overhang the ends of the two Back Supports (E) by ½ inch. Apply glue to the meeting surfaces, and screw through the Back (F) into

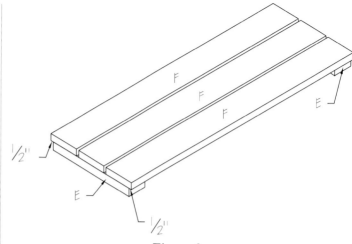

Figure 3

each of the Back Supports (E), using two 2-inch wood screws on each joint.

5. Repeat step 4 twice (without the ½-inch overhang) to attach the remaining two Backs (F) to the two Back Supports (E).

Making the Sides

1. Cut two Arms (G) from 1 x 4 pine, each measuring 26 inches.

2. Using figure 4 as a guide, shape one Arm (G), eliminating the shaded portions. Use the resulting Arm (G) as a pattern to shape the remaining Arm (G).

3. Cut four Arm Supports (H) from 2 x 4 pine, each measuring 11½ inches.

4. Place the seat assembly (A, B, C, and D) on a level surface. Position the four Arm Supports

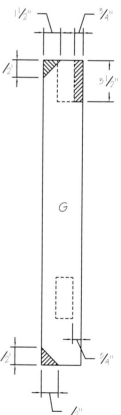

Figure 4

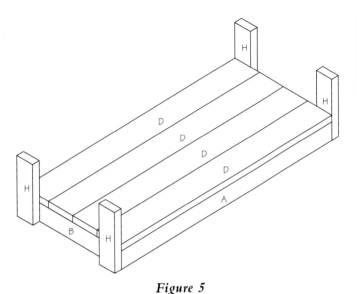

Figure 5

(H) on end at each of the four corners of the seat assembly, as shown in figure 5. The Arm Supports (H) should be flush with the Seat Front/Backs (A) at the front and back of the assembly. Screw through the Arm Supports (H) into the Seat Front/Backs (A), using a 2½-inch wood screw. To reinforce the joint, insert a 3½-inch lag bolt through the Arm Support (H) and the Seat Sides (B). Tighten the bolt securely. Repeat the procedure to attach the remaining three Arm Supports (H).

5. Using figure 4 as a placement guide (see page 53), place one Arm (G) over the ends of the two Arm Supports (H). The rear Arm Support (H) should be flush against the 3½- x ¾-inch cutout in the Arm (G), and the front Arm Support (H) should be ¾ inch from the same edge. Apply glue to the meeting surfaces, and screw through the Arm (G) into the Arm Support (H), using one 2½-inch wood screw on each joint.

Adding the Back

1. Insert the back assembly between the two assembled arms. The Backs (F) should face the front of the swing, and the exposed portion of the two Back Supports (E) should be against the seat. The back assembly will be secured to the rear Arm Supports (H). To make the swing more comfortable, tilt the back assembly at a slight

angle—out at the top and in at the bottom. The tilt angle is determined by the width of the 2 x 4 on the Arm Supports (H).

2. When you have the back fitted perfectly, secure the assembly with bar clamps. Screw through the Arm Supports (H) into the Back Supports (E), using two 2½-inch wood screws. Then insert two 3½-inch lag screws through each of the Arm Supports (H) into the Back Supports (E).

Finishing

1. Fill any cracks, crevices, and screw holes with wood filler.

2. Sand the completed swing thoroughly.

3. Paint or stain the swing the color of your choice—or simply leave it the natural color.

4. Screw a 3-inch eye bolt through the top of the Arm (G) into both the front and rear Arm Supports (H) on both sides of the swing.

5. Hang the swing using heavy-duty chain. Make certain that the structure you hang it from can support the weight.

6. Mix up a pitcher of lemonade, and enjoy!

We have made many Adirondack chairs over the years and thought it would be neat to have one that was just a bit larger. So this time we built a good-sized bench. Whether you share the bench with a friend or stretch out on it all by yourself, you will enjoy the traditional Adirondack shape.

Materials

30 linear feet of 1 x 6 pine

56 linear feet of 1 x 4 pine

5 linear feet of 1 x 2 pine

5 linear feet of 2 x 4 pine

Hardware

50 1⅝" wood screws

15 1¼" (3d) finish nails

60 1¼" wood screws

2 carriage bolts, ⅜" x 3", with washer and nut

Special Tools and Techniques

C clamp

Bar clamp (optional)

Cutting List

Code	Description	Qty.	Materials	Dimensions
A	Seat Brace	3	1 x 6 pine	39" long
B	Front Seat Trim	1	1 x 6 pine	46" long
C	Seat Side	2	1 x 4 pine	24" long
D	Seat Slat	6	1 x 4 pine	46" long
E	Back Slat	12	1 x 4 pine	32" long
F	Back Support	2	1 x 2 pine	46" long
G	Arm	2	1 x 6 pine	27" long
H	Arm Connector	1	2 x 4 pine	52" long
I	Arm Brace	2	1 x 4 pine	9" long

Making the Seat

1. The trademark of the Adirondack sofa is the angled seat. The braces that support the seat are simple to construct but must be cut to the exact dimensions to work. Cut three Seat Braces (A) from 1 x 6 pine, each measuring 39 inches. To achieve the necessary angles for the Seat Braces (A), refer to figure 1. Portions of the Seat Braces (A) must be cut away. This is as simple as "connect the letters." Following the measurements in figure 1, label each point, then draw a straight line from a to b, b to c, d to e, and e to f. Cut along the lines you have just drawn to eliminate the shaded portions of one Seat Brace (A), as shown in figure 1. Use the resulting Seat Brace (A) as a pattern to cut the other two Seat Braces (A).

2. Cut one Front Seat Trim (B) from 1 x 6 pine, measuring 46 inches.

3. The Front Seat Trim (B) will be used to connect the three Seat Braces (A). Position two

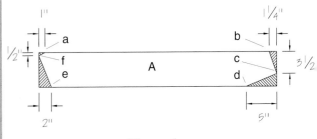

Figure 1

Seat Braces (A) parallel to each other and on edge, with the e-f edge facing up, 44½ inches apart. Fit the Front Seat Trim (B) over the e-f edge, as shown in figure 2. Screw through the Front Seat Trim (B) into the ends of the Seat Braces (A), using two 1⅝-inch wood screws on each joint. Center the third Seat Brace (A) between the two far Seat Braces (A), and screw through the Front Seat Trim (B) into the center Seat Brace (A), using 1⅝-inch wood screws (see figure 2).

4. Cut two Seat Sides (C) from 1 x 4 pine, each measuring 24 inches.

5. Turn the assembly right side up. Using figure 3 as a guide, attach the Seat Sides (C) to the Seat Braces (A), 6 inches from the top edge of the Seat Sides (C) and flush with the Seat Trim (B) on the front. Drill a ⅜-inch-diameter hole through each seat side (c) and seat brace (a), spacing the bolts about 3 inches apart. Secure the joint by slipping a 2-inch carriage bolt through the holes, and tighten the bolts with washers and nuts.

Adding the Seat Slats

1. Cut six Seat Slats (D) from 1 x 4 pine, each measuring 46 inches.

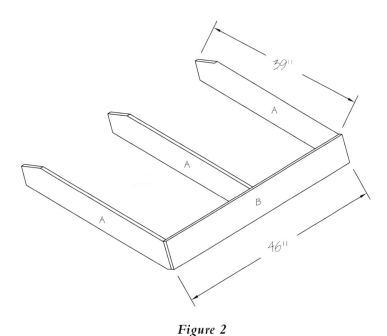

Figure 2

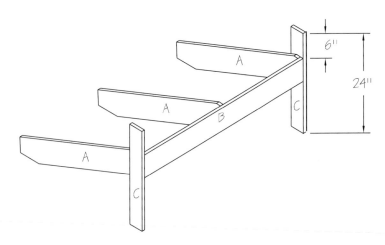

Figure 3

2. For comfort, round off the long edge of one of the Seat Slats (D), which will be attached to the front of the bench. Attach this Seat Slat (D) to the f-a edge of the Seat Braces (A) so that it extends 1⅜ inches over the Seat Trim (B), as shown in figure 4. Use two 1¼-inch finish nails on each side, and four 1¼-inch finish nails spaced evenly across the front.

3. Attach the next four Seat Slats (D) to the Seat Braces (A), as shown in figure 4, spacing them approximately ⅜ inch apart. Use two 1⅝-inch wood screws on each joint. Attach the sixth Seat Slat (D) 2 inches from the fifth

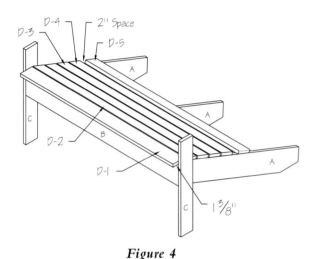

Figure 4

Seat Slat (D). (This extra space will be needed later to accommodate the back of the bench.)

Constructing the Back

1. Cut 12 Back Slats (E) from 1 x 4 pine, measuring 32 inches.

2. Cut two Back Supports (F) from 1 x 2 pine, each measuring 46 inches.

3. Place the two Back Supports (F) on a level surface, parallel to each other and 24 inches apart.

4. Place the 12 Back Slats (E) on top of the two Back Supports (F), spaced evenly approximately ⅜ inch apart, as shown in figure 5. Make sure that the Back Slats (E) are square to the Back Supports (F). Note that the ends of all

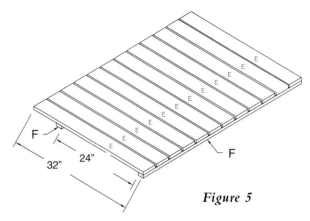

Figure 5

of the Back Slats (E) are even with one Back Support (F) at what will be the lower bench back. Screw through each of the Back Slats (E) into each of the Back Supports (F). Use two 1¼-inch wood screws at each joint.

5. Using figure 6 as a guide, cut off the two outer corners of the assembled back.

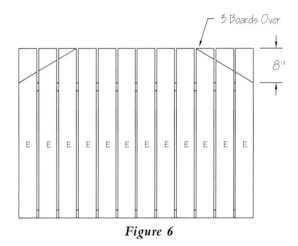

Figure 6

Constructing the Arm Assembly

1. Cut two Arms (G) from 1 x 6 pine, each measuring 27 inches.

2. Using figure 7 as a guide, remove the shaded portions from one Arm (G) in the same manner as you cut the Seat Braces (A) (see figure 1). Use this Arm (G) as a pattern to cut the other Arm (G).

3. Cut one Arm Connector (H) from 2 x 4 pine, measuring 52 inches.

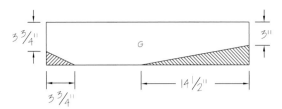

Figure 7

4. In order to accommodate the back of the bench, one edge of the Arm Connector (H) must be angled. Rip the arm connector (H), roughly 33° along its length, as shown in figure 8.

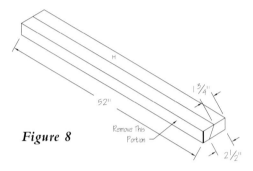

Figure 8

5. Place the two Arms (G) over the ends of the Arm Connector (H). Make certain that the space between the two Arms (G) is just slightly more than 46 inches in order to accommodate the back assembly. Clamp the two Arms (G) to the ends of the Arm Connector (H), using C clamps.

Final Assembly

1. Although you can perform this assembly with the assistance of bar clamps, it is easier to enlist the aid of a helper. First, fit the back assembly into the 2-inch-wide gap in the seat slats, with the back slats facing the front of the bench, as shown in figure 9. Then wrap the clamped arm assembly around the back of the bench so that the front of the Arm (G) rests on the bench sides. Have the helper sit in the bench, then adjust the clamped arm assembly so that the Arms (G) are level to the floor and the back of the bench is at the most comfortable angle. Screw through the Arms (G) to secure them to the bench sides, using two 1¼-inch wood screws on each joint. Mark the placement of the Arm Connector (H) on the back assembly

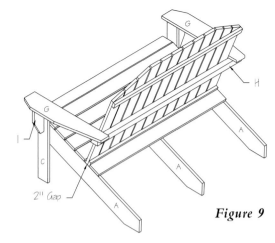

Figure 9

2. Screw through each of the Back Slats (E) into the Arm Connector (H). Use two 1¼-inch wood screws on each joint.

3. Drill a ⅜-inch-diameter hole in each Arm (G) through the Arm Connector (H), and secure the joint by inserting a 3-inch carriage bolt through the drilled holes. Add a washer and a nut, and tighten the bolt securely.

4. Cut two Arm Braces (I) from 1 x 4 pine, each measuring 9 inches. Using figure 10 as a guide, remove the shaded portion of one of the Arm Braces (I). Use this Arm Brace (I) as a pattern to mark and cut the second Arm Brace (I).

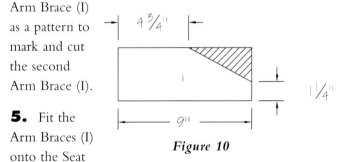

Figure 10

5. Fit the Arm Braces (I) onto the Seat Sides (C), under the arms, with the 9-inch edge facing the Seat Sides (C), as shown in figure 9. Screw through the Seat Sides (C) and Arms (G) into the Arm Braces (I), using two or three 1⅝-inch wood screws on each joint.

Finishing

1. Fill any screw holes with wood filler. Sand all surfaces thoroughly. (Remember that people will be sitting on this project, so you will want a very smooth surface.)

2. Let the sofa weather naturally or stain it the color of your choice.

Portable Deck

If you have always wanted an outdoor deck but are renting or not planning to live in your house very long, this portable deck is the answer. It also has the advantage of being built in squares that can be arranged, rearranged, or moved. So when you leave that apartment or rental house, this handy deck goes on the moving truck with you!

Materials

22 linear feet of 2 x 6 pine

35 linear feet of ¾ x 6 pine decking

3 linear feet of 4 x 4 pine

Hardware

28 3½" wood screws

55 2½" wood screws

Cutting List (for one square)

Code	Description	Qty.	Materials	Dimensions
A	Short Side	3	2 x 6 pine	43" long
B	Long Side	2	2 x 6 pine	46" long
C	Top	8	¾ x 6 pine	46" long
D	Leg	4	4 x 4 pine	7½" long

Building the Frame

1. Cut three Short Sides (A) from 2 x 6 pine, each measuring 43 inches.

2. Cut two Long Sides (B) from 2 x 6 pine, each measuring 46 inches.

3. Position two of the Short Sides (A) on edge, parallel to each other and 43 inches apart. Place the two Long Sides (B) over the ends of the Short Sides (A), as shown in figure 1 (page 64). Apply glue to the meeting surfaces, and nail through the Long Sides (B) into the ends of the Short Sides (A), using two 3½-inch wood screws on each joint.

4. Place the third Short Side (A) between the two Long Sides (b) and parallel to the Short Sides (A), as shown in figure 1. Apply glue to the meeting surfaces, and screw through the face of the Long Side (B) into the end of the Short Side (A), using two 3½-inch wood screws on each joint.

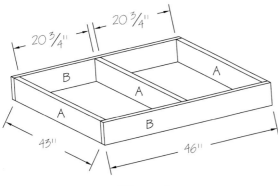

Figure 1

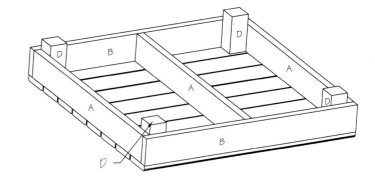

Figure 3

Adding the Decking

1. Cut eight Tops (C) from ¾ x 6 pine decking, each measuring 46 inches.

2. Place the Tops (C) over one side of the assembled frame so that the boards lay perpendicular to the Short Sides (A), as shown in figure 2. Screw through the face of the deck boards into the edges of all three Short Sides (A), using two 2½-inch wood screws per joist.

Finishing

1. Sand the edges of your deck square.

2. Paint, stain, or seal square as desired.

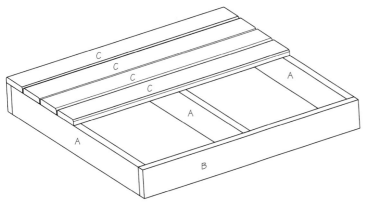

Figure 2

Adding the Legs

1. Cut four Legs (D) from 4 x 4 pine, each measuring 7½ inches.

2. Turn the assembled frame and decking over so that the decking is on the bottom. Place the four Legs (D) in each corner, as shown in figure 3, and secure each in place, using two 3½-inch wood screws in each Short Side (A) and each Long Side (B).

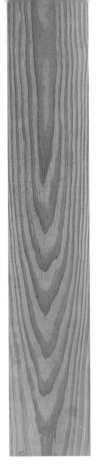

Deck Canopy

··

Until we built this canopy, we could not use most of our deck during the heat of the day. Now we can enjoy the outdoor space all day. The canvas panels shade the entire deck or can be pulled back if you want to feel more of the warmth of the sun.

Building the Frame

1. Dig two holes approximately 116 inches apart from the center of the hole and 118 inches away from your house to the depth of about 3 feet or to the depth your local building code specifies.

2. Cut two Posts (A) from 4 x 4 pressure-treated pine, each measuring 16 feet. Place one Post (A) in each hole and set in place, using a bag of mixed concrete for each Post (A). Make

sure that both posts are plumb. Secure Posts (A) temporarily by using a bracing board on two sides of the posts. Let cement set up overnight.

3. Cut 2 Roof Supports (B) from 2 x 6 pine, each measuring 143 inches long. For a decorative (but optional) touch, miter both ends of the Roof Supports (B) at opposing 30° angles, as shown in figure 1 (page 68).

*Notes on Construction and Materials

We suggest that, before starting this project, you consult local building codes. We also suggest obtaining the appropriate construction permits before you begin, since this project will be attached to your home. Because every house is different, make certain that the chosen height and distance from the house will work with your structure. Also, the pitch of your roof may make a difference in how some of the project pieces are attached.

This project will require a professional to cut the pipe to length and thread the ends. Most home centers will do this for a minimal charge.

Materials

32 linear feet of 4 x 4 pressure-treated pine

2 50-pound bags of concrete

65 linear feet of 2 x 6 pine

4 6' lengths of ¾"-diameter galvanized pipe, threaded on both ends★

8 1" lengths of ¾"-diameter galvanized pipe, threaded on both ends★

8 galvanized pipe flanges to fit ¾"-diameter pipe

8 90° pipe angles to fit ¾"-diameter pipe

2 canvas panels, each 54" x 72", hemmed on all four sides, with grommets
     inserted every foot along the 72" lengths

Hardware

10 2½" wood screws

4 3½" lag bolts

6 galvanized metal tie-down braces

40 1¼" wood screws

32 metal shower curtain rings

Special Tools and Techniques

Miter (optional)

Cutting List

Code	Description	Qty.	Materials	Dimensions
A	Post	2	4 x 4 pine	16' long
B	Roof Supports	2	2 x 6 pine	143" long
C	Tops	3	2 x 6 pine	144" long

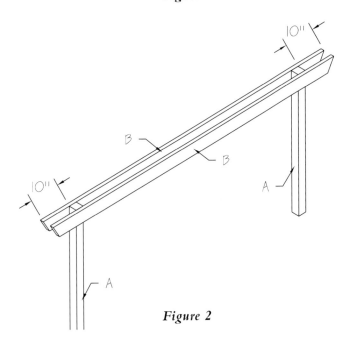

Figure 1

2. Place the three Tops (C) on edge over the Roof Supports (B), with the mitered end away from the house, as shown in figure 3. Attach the Tops (C) to the Roof Supports (B) with metal tie-down braces. Make sure that the Tops (C) are level before installing the braces.

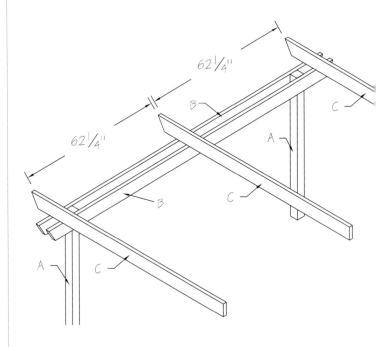

Figure 2

4. This step requires the use of two ladders or two really tall people. Mark the distance to the required height to match the shingled edge of your roof from the ground or deck. Place one Roof Support (B) over one side of the Posts (A), as shown in figure 2. Screw through the Roof Support (B) into the Posts (A). Temporarily hold the pieces together with two 2½-inch wood screws in each post, then install one 3½-inch lag bolt on each Post (A).

5. Repeat step 4 to attach the remaining Roof Support (B) to the other side of the Posts (A). This will sandwich the two Posts (A) between the two Roof Supports (B).

Adding the Tops

1. Cut three Tops (C) from 2 x 6 pine, each measuring 144 inches long. If desired, use a miter to make a 30° cut on one end of each of the Tops (C).

Figure 3

3. Attach the ends of the Tops (C) on top of the roof in the same manner, making sure that any relevant code requirements are followed explicitly. Use the same braces as used to connect the Tops (C) to the Roof Support (B).

Adding the Pipe

1. Attach, in the following order, the 90° pipe corner to the long pipe, then the 1-inch-long pipe to the other side of the 90° corner, then the flange to the 1-inch-long pipe, which will allow you to screw the flange to the Top (C).

2. Repeat step 2 with the opposite end and the remaining pipes.

Installation

1. Install the pipes 10 inches away from the end of the Tops (C), as shown in figure 4.

2. Attach the canvas to the pipes, using shower curtain rings.

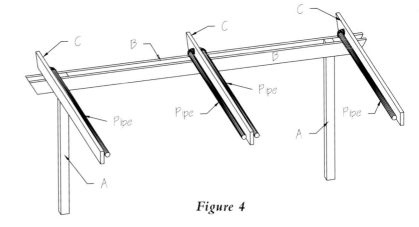

Figure 4

Barbecue Table

If you have arrived at your barbecue with hands full of sauces, steaks, tongs, hot pads, and spatulas and had nowhere to put them, you'll want to build this barbecue table. It's perfectly sized to hold trays and bottles, and even has a place to hang your barbecue tools.

Materials

12 linear feet of 2 x 2 pine

30 linear feet of 1 x 4 pine

10 linear feet of ¾ x 6 pine

Hardware

16 1⅝" wood screws

36 2" wood screws

50 1¼" (3d) finish nails

3 cup hooks

Cutting List

Code	Description	Qty.	Material	Dimension
A	Long Side	4	1 x 4 pine	34½" long
B	Short Side	4	1 x 4 pine	15" long
C	Leg	4	2 x 2 pine	32" long
D	Support Trim	2	1 x 1 pine	32¾" long
E	Shelf Board	8	1 x 4 pine	13½" long
F	Top Support	1	1 x 4 pine	13½" long
G	Top Boards	3	¾ x 6 pine	38" long

Making the Frame

1. Cut four Long Sides (A) from 1 x 4 pine, each measuring 34½ inches.

2. Cut four Short Sides (B) from 1 x 4 pine, each measuring 15 inches.

3. Place two of the Long Sides (A) on edge, parallel to each other, and 13½ inches apart. Fit two of the Short Sides (B) over the ends of the Long Sides (A) to form a rectangle measuring 36 x 15 inches, as shown in figure 1. Apply glue to the meeting surfaces, and screw through the face of the Short Sides (B) into the ends of the Long Sides (A), using 1⅝-inch wood screws.

4. Repeat step 3 to form another rectangle with the remaining two Short and Long Sides (A and B). Designate one rectangle as the "Top" and the other as the "Bottom."

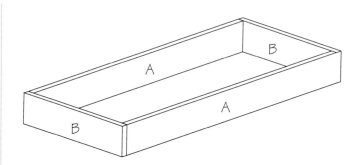

Figure 1

5. Cut four Legs (C) from 2 x 2 pine, each measuring 32 inches.

6. Place the four Legs (C) inside the corners of the assembled rectangle designated "Top," as shown in figure 2 (page 72). Apply glue to the meeting surfaces, and screw through the Short and Long Sides (A and B) into both sides of each Leg (C), using two 2-inch wood screws on each joint.

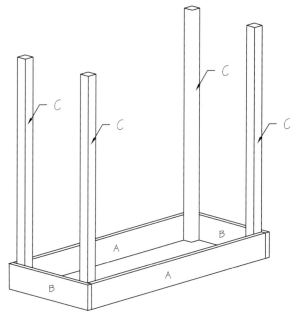

Figure 2

7. Place the assembled rectangle designated "Bottom" over the four Legs (C), 12 inches below the Top, as shown in figure 3. Again, apply glue to the meeting surfaces, and screw through the Short and Long Sides (A and B) into both sides of each Leg (C), using two 2-inch wood screws on each joint.

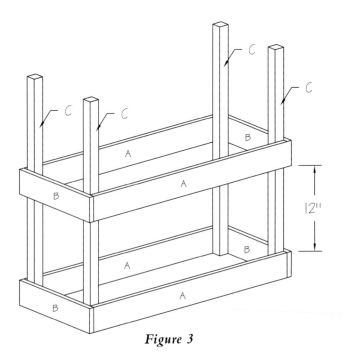

Figure 3

Adding the Bottom Shelf

1. Cut two Support Trims (D) from 1 x 1 pine, each measuring 32¾ inches.

2. Cut eight Shelf Boards (E) from 1 x 4 pine, each measuring 13½ inches.

3. Place the Support Trims (D) inside the Long Sides (A) of the Bottom rectangle, ¾ inch from the top edge of the Long Sides (A), as shown in figure 4. Apply glue to the meeting surfaces, and nail through the Support Trims (D) into the Long Sides (A), using 1¼-inch finish nails evenly spaced about 3 inches apart.

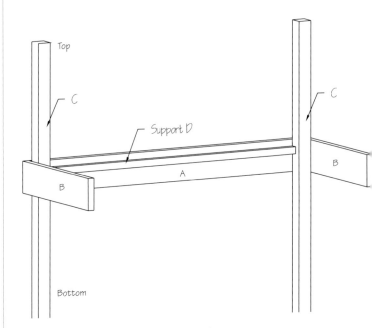

Figure 4

4. Place the eight Shelf Boards (E) between the Long Sides (A) over the Support Trims (D), as shown in figure 5. Space the Shelf Boards (E) approximately ½ inch apart. Apply glue to the meeting surfaces, and nail through the Shelf Boards (E) into the Support Trims (D), using two 1¼-inch finish nails on each joint.

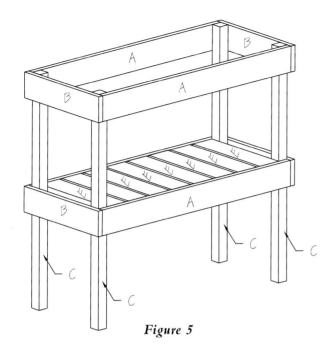

Figure 5

Adding the Top

1. Cut one Top Support (F) from 1 x 4 pine, measuring 13½ inches.

2. Place the Top Support (F) between the two Long Sides (A) on the Top, centered between the two Short Sides (B), as shown in figure 6. Apply glue to the meeting surfaces, and screw through the Long Sides (A), using two 1⅞-inch wood screws on each joint.

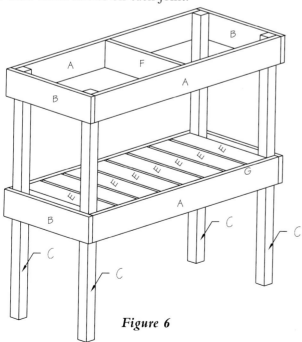

Figure 6

3. Cut three Top Boards (G) from ¾ x 6 deck boards, each measuring 38 inches.

4. Place the three Top Boards (G) over the Top, as shown in figure 7. The Top Boards (G) will overhang the Top by 1 inch on all four sides. Apply glue to the meeting surfaces, and nail through the Top Boards (G) into the Long Sides (A), Short Sides (B), and Top Support (F), using two 2-inch wood screws on each joint.

Figure 7

Finishing

1. Fill any cracks or crevices with wood filler and sand the table thoroughly.

2. Paint or stain the table the color of your choice, or leave the wood natural. The bottom of this table has been stained a natural color, and the top was painted red. We have lettered "Let's Get Cookin'" on the bottom side of the finished tabletop.

3. Screw three cup hooks to one end of the tabletop for hanging barbecue tools.

Who doesn't need a sturdy picnic table? We use ours just about every weekend when friends come to visit. This one has a checkerboard painted on it—our young friends love to play "shell" checkers on it with shells they collected on the beach. The benches stand alone as super garden seating.

Materials

For the picnic table:

28 linear feet of 2 x 4 pine

27 linear feet of 1 x 6 pine

For one bench:

15 linear feet of 2 x 10 pine

Hardware

8 3½" carriage bolts with matching washers and nuts

30 2" wood screws

25 2½" wood screws

Special Tools and Techniques

Miter

Cutting List

Code	Description	Qty.	Materials	Dimensions
A	Leg	4	2 x 4 pine	37" long
B	Leg Support	2	2 x 4 pine	17¾" long
C	Top	5	1 x 6 pine	60" long
D	Top Support	3	2 x 4 pine	27½" long
E	Brace	2	2 x 4 pine	25" long
F	Bench Leg	2	2 x 10 pine	16" long
G	Bench Top	1	2 x 10 pine	60" long
H	Bench Brace	2	2 x 10 pine	7" long

Making the Legs

1. Cut four Legs (A) from 2 x 4 pine, each measuring 37 inches long.

2. Using figure 1 as a guide, trim the ends of each Leg (A), and drill a ½-inch-diameter hole in the center.

3. Position two Legs (A), one on top of the other, to form an X, aligning the two center holes. Insert a 3½-inch carriage bolt through the center holes and add a matching washer and nut. Adjust the Legs (A) so that the upper and lower outer measurement of the Legs (A) is 22½ inches, as shown in figure 2.

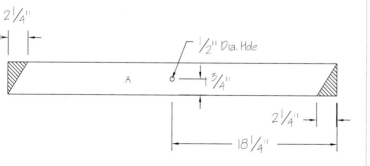

Figure 1

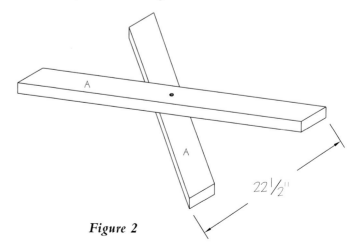

Figure 2

4. Repeat step 3 to form another X-shaped assembly with the remaining two Legs (A).

5. Cut two Leg Supports (B) from 2 x 4 pine, each measuring 17¾ inches.

6. Using figure 3 as a guide, trim both ends of each Leg Support (B).

Figure 3

7. Position one X-shaped assembly flat on a work surface, with the carriage bolt head on the underside. Place one Leg Support (B) flush with the top ends of the X-shaped assembly, as shown in figure 4. Note that the Leg Support (B) overlaps the lower Leg (A), and butts against the upper Leg (A).

8. Repeat step 7 to attach the remaining Leg Support (B) to the remaining X-shaped assembly.

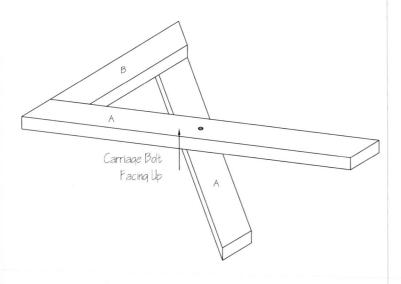

Figure 4

Making the Top

1. Cut five Tops (C) from 1 x 6 pine, each measuring 60 inches.

2. Cut three Top Supports (D) from 2 x 4 pine, each measuring 27½ inches.

3. Using figure 3 as a guide, trim the corners on each of the three Top Supports (D).

4. Position three Top Supports (D) on a level surface (trimmed edges down), parallel to each other and 22¼ inches apart. Place the five Tops (C) over the three Top Supports (D), as shown in figure 5. Make certain that the assembly is square. Screw through the Tops (C) into each of the three Top Supports (D), using two 2-inch wood screws on each joint.

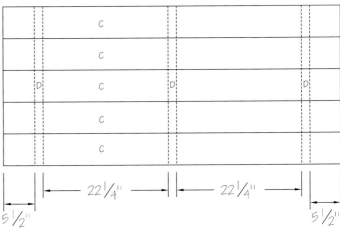

Figure 5

Final Table Assembly

1. Turn the top assembly (Tops [C] and Top Supports [D]) upside down on a level surface. Position one X-shaped assembly so that the Leg Support (B) is flush against the inner surface of the Top Support (D), as shown in figure 6. Apply glue to the meeting surfaces, and screw through the Top Support (D) into the Leg Support (B), using two 2½-inch wood screws. This will hold the assembly together temporarily.

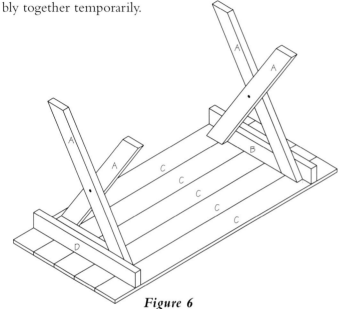

Figure 6

2. Drill two ½-inch-diameter holes through the Leg Support (B) and the Top Support (D), using figure 7 as a guide for exact placement.

3. Drill one ½-inch-diameter hole through the Leg (A) and the Top Support (D). Again, refer to figure 7 for exact placement.

4. Insert a 3½-inch carriage bolt through each of the three drilled holes, add the nut, and tighten.

5. Repeat steps 1 through 4 to attach the remaining X-shaped assembly and Leg Support (A) to the top assembly.

6. Cut two Braces (E) from 2 x 4 pine, each measuring 25 inches.

7. Miter the ends of each Brace (E) at opposing 45° angles, as shown in figure 8.

Figure 8

8. Position the brace (short edge down) so that one mitered end is against the center of the X-shaped assembly and the opposite end is against the Tops (C), as shown in figure 9. Screw at an angle through the Brace (E) into the X-shaped assembly, using one 2½-inch wood screw.

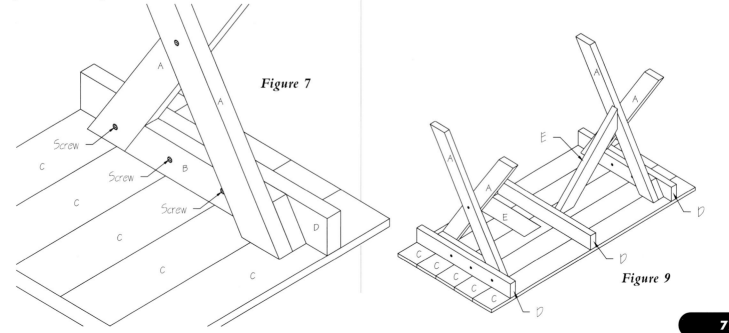

Figure 7

Figure 9

9. Repeat step 8 to attach the remaining Brace (E) to the opposite side of the table.

10. Carefully turn the entire assembly right side up, and screw through the center Top (C) into the unattached end of the Brace (E), using two 2½-inch wood screws.

11. Repeat step 10 to secure the remaining unattached Brace (E) to the center Top (C) on the opposite side of the table.

Making the Bench

1. Cut two Bench Legs (A) from 2 x 10 pine, each measuring 16 inches.

2. Referring to the placement measurements given in figure 10, drill a 1¼-inch-diameter hole centered horizontally and 7⅜ inches from one end of a Bench Leg (F).

3. Again referring to figure 10, cut away the center portion of the Bench Leg (F) to form an inverted V shape.

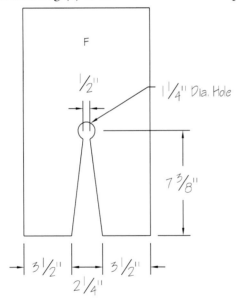

Figure 10

4. Repeat steps 2 and 3 to cut out the remaining Bench Leg (F).

5. Cut one Bench Top (G) from 2 x 10 pine, measuring 60 inches.

6. Position the two Bench Legs (F) on edge with the cutout against the work surface, parallel to each other and 45 inches apart. Place the Bench Top (G) over the Bench Legs (F). The Bench Top (G) should overhang each of the Bench Legs (F) by 6 inches. Screw through the Bench Top (G) into each of the Bench Legs (F), using three 2½-inch wood screws.

7. Cut two Bench Braces (H) from 2 x 10 pine, each measuring 7 inches.

8. Miter the ends of the Bench Braces (H) at opposing 45° angles, as shown in figure 11.

9. Turn the bench assembly upside down. Fit the

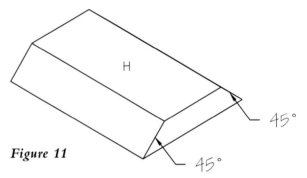

Figure 11

mitered Bench Braces (H) between the Bench Legs (F) and Bench Top (G), as shown in figure 12. Apply glue to the meeting surfaces, and screw at an angle through the Bench Braces (H) into both the Bench Top (G) and Bench Legs (F), using three 2½-inch wood screws on each joint.

10. If you want two benches, you will need to repeat the entire procedure.

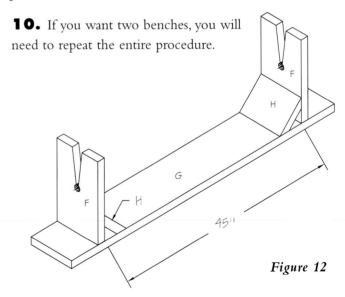

Figure 12

Finishing

1. Sand the entire picnic table and bench.

2. Painting a checkerboard pattern on the top of the picnic table will double its use. A checkerboard is easy to do—we simply drew eight rows of eight 2-inch squares in the center of the table and painted the squares alternating colors. We left the remainder of the table its natural color.

Trash Container

I t is nice to have a trash container that is pretty enough to place near the outdoor eating area. We developed this simple, yet attractive—not to mention easy-to-construct—project when we got tired of having to walk our trash around the house to the back of the garage.

Materials

28 linear feet of 1 x 4 pine

12 linear feet of 2 x 2 pine

4' x 4' sheet of privacy lattice

10 linear feet of 1½" L-shaped molding

2' x 2' sheet of ¾" plywood

Fence-post finial

Hardware

50 1⅝" wood screws

340 1¼" (3d) finish nails

Cutting List

Code	Description	Qty.	Materials	Dimensions
A	Long Side	4	1 x 4 pine	24½" long
B	Short Side	4	1 x 4 pine	23" long
C	Support	4	2 x 2 pine	28" long
D	Sides	4	Lattice	24" x 21"
E	Corner Trim	4	L-molding	24" long
F	Short Trim	2	1 x 4 pine	17½" long
G	Long Trim	2	1 x 4 pine	24½" long
H	Lid	1	¾" plywood	22½" x 22½"
I	Lid Center	1	1 x 4 pine	3½" x 3½"

Building the Frame

1. Cut four Long Sides (A) from 1 x 4 pine, each measuring 24½ inches.

2. Cut four Short Sides (B) from 1 x 4 pine, each measuring 23 inches.

3. Cut four Supports (C) from 2 x 2 pine, each measuring 28 inches.

4. Position two of the Short Sides (B), parallel to each other on edge and 23 inches apart. Place two of the Long Sides (A) over the ends of Short Sides (B), as shown in figure 1, to form a square. Apply glue to the meeting surfaces, and screw through the Long Sides (A) into the Short Sides (B), using two 1⅝-inch wood screws in each joint.

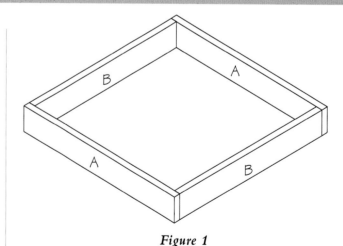

Figure 1

5. Repeat step 4 to assemble another square, using the remaining Short (A) and Long (B) Sides. Designate one as "Top" and one as "Bottom."

6. Place the Bottom square flat on a level surface and attach the Supports (C) to the inside corners of the

Bottom square, as shown in figure 2. Apply glue to the meeting surfaces, and screw through the Short and Long sides (A and B) into the Supports (C), using four 1⅝-inch wood screws in each joint.

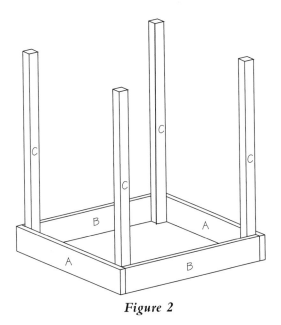

Figure 2

7. Repeat step 6 to attach the Top square to the exposed supports, as shown in figure 3.

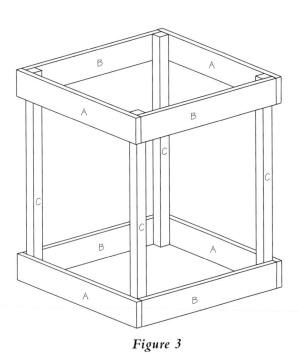

Figure 3

Adding the Lattice

1. Cut four Sides (D) from privacy lattice, each measuring 24 x 21 inches.

2. Attach the Sides (D) by laying the assembly on its side and placing the Sides (D) between the Top and Bottom squares and over the Supports (C). Nail through the Sides (D) into the Supports (C), using about five 1¼-inch finish nails per Support (C).

3. Cut four Corner Trims (E) from 1½-inch L-Shaped molding, each measuring 24 inches.

4. Place the Corner Trims (E) over the corners of the frame, and nail through the Corner Trims (E) and through the lattice into the Supports (C), using about five 1¼-inch nails per Side (D).

Making the Top

1. Cut two Short Trims (F) from 1 x 4 pine, each measuring 17½ inches.

2. Cut two Long Trims (G) from 1 x 4 pine, each measuring 24½ inches.

3. Cut one Lid (H) from 3/4-inch plywood, measuring 22½ x 22½ inches.

4. Position the two Short Trims (F) flat on a level surface, parallel to each other and 17½ inches apart. Place the Long Trims (G) against the ends of the Short Trims (F), as shown in figure 4. Position the Lid (H), centered over the Trims (F and G) so that they extend 1 inch beyond the Lid (H), as shown in figure 5. Apply glue to the meeting surfaces, and nail through the Lid (H) into the Trims (F and G), using 1¼-inch finish nails spaced about every 4 inches.

5. Cut one Lid Center (I) from 1 x 4 pine, measuring 3½ x 3½ inches.

6. Turn the assembled lid over, so that Lid (H) is on the bottom and the Trims (F and G) are facing up. Using

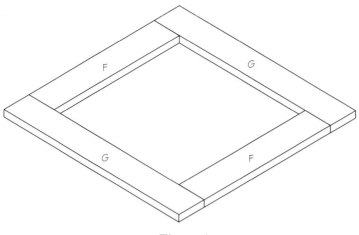

Figure 4

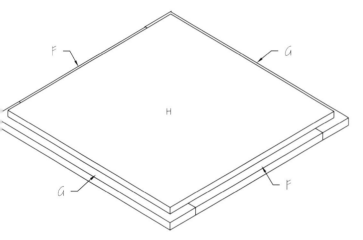

Figure 5

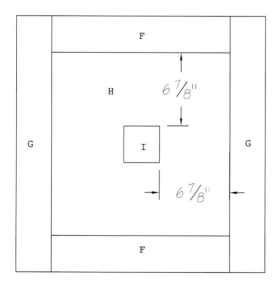

Figure 6

figure 6 as a guide, place the Lid Center (I) on the Lid (H). Apply glue to the meeting surfaces, and nail through the Lid Center (I) into the Lid (H), using four 1¼-inch finish nails. Note: Do not nail into the center of the Lid Center (I), but rather nail an inch inside the corners of the Lid Center (I). The finial will be attached to the Lid Center (I) in the next step.

7. Drill into the Lid Center (I), using an ⅛-inch drill bit, making sure to center the hole in the Lid Center (H). Screw the finial into the Lid Center (I).

Finishing

1. Sand the container thoroughly and fill any cracks or crevices with wood filler

2. Paint or stain the container the color of your choice, or leave it natural.

Arbor

Every garden needs an arbor. This one is positioned over a walkway in the yard to serve as a pleasant transition from one outdoor living area to another; it would also be at home over a entryway gate or in a corner of the yard. Plant a fast-growing vine at the base of the arbor, and you'll have a beautiful addition to your garden.

Materials

32 linear feet of 2 x 2 pine

4' x 8' sheet of privacy lattice

10 linear feet of 1 x 6 pine

15 linear feet of 2 x 4 pine

Hardware

80 1¼" (3d) finish nails

15 1⅝" wood screws

12 2" wood screws

Special Tools and Techniques

Dado

Cutting List

Code	Description	Qty.	Materials	Dimensions
A	Side	4	2 x 2 pine	90" long
B	Panel	2	Privacy Lattice	12" x 80"
C	Support	2	1 x 6 pine	48" long
D	Top	5	2 x 4 pine	33" long

Building the Side Frames

1. Cut four Sides (A) from 2 x 2 pine, each measuring 90 inches long.

2. Cut two Panels (B) from lattice, each measuring 12 x 80 inches.

3. Cut a dado, ¾ inch wide and ½ inch deep, down the length of the Sides (A), as shown in figure 1.

4. Place one Panel (B) inside one Side (A) dado. The Panel (B) should be even with one end of the Side (A), as shown in figure 2. Apply glue to the dado, and toenail through the Panel (B) into the Side (A), using 1¼-inch finish nails spaced about every 5 inches.

5. Repeat step 4 to attach the other Side (A) to the opposite edge of the Panel (B).

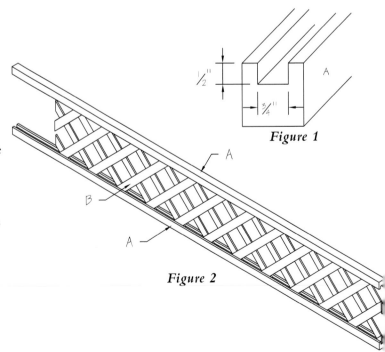

Figure 1

Figure 2

6. Assemble a second frame, using the remaining two Sides (A) and the remaining Panel (B).

Adding the Top

1. Cut two Supports (C) from 1 x 6 pine, each measuring 48 inches long.

2. Using figure 3 as a guide, cut off two of the corners on both Supports (C).

Figure 3

3. Cut five Tops (D) from 2 x 4 pine, each measuring 33 inches long. Using figure 4 as a guide, cut the ends of the Tops (D) at an angle.

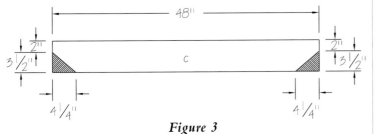

Figure 4

4. Place the two assembled frames on edge, parallel to each other, and 34 inches apart. Place one Support (C) over the flush ends of the assembled frames, as shown in figure 5. The edge of the Support (C) should be even with the ends of the Sides (A). Apply glue to the meeting surfaces, and screw through the Support (C), using three 1⅝-inch screws on each joint.

5. Repeat step 4 to attach the remaining Support (C).

6. Install the arbor in its final spot outside, making sure that the legs are level and plumb. The Sides (A) that extend beyond the Panel (B) should be below ground level.

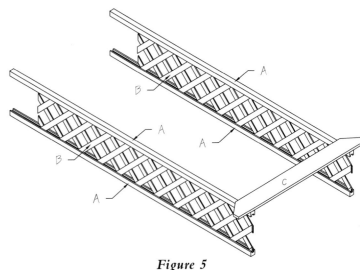

Figure 5

7. Position the five Tops (D) in place, perpendicular to the Supports (C), as shown in figure 6. Screw through the Supports (C) at an angle into the Tops (D), using 2-inch screws.

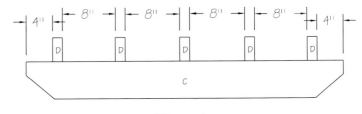

Figure 6

Finishing

1. Sand the completed arbor thoroughly.

2. Either paint or stain the arbor the color of your choice or simply leave it natural.

Outdoor Bar

You are sure to be the "hostess with the mostest" at your next party when you outfit this outdoor bar with a choice of beverages. The bar is great for outdoor entertaining, since it keeps the beverage service out of the kitchen.

Materials

4' x 8' sheet of ¾" plywood

16 linear feet of 2 x 2 pine

4 decorative 4 x 4 posts, at least 45" long

21 linear feet of 2 x 4 pine

10 linear feet of 1 x 2 pine

4' x 4' sheet of lattice

4"-wide top rail, 5' long

16 square feet of tile

1 qt. ceramic tile adhesive

7 lb. sanded grout, in color of your choice

Small bottle of silicone grout sealer

Hardware

25 1⅝" wood screws

40 2½" wood screws

35 2" wood screws

10 2" (6d) finish nails

20 1¼" (3d) finish nails

30 1" (2d) finish nails

Special Tools and Techniques

Bar clamps

Miter

⅛" V trowel

Rubber tile float

Cutting List

Code	Description	Qty.	Materials	Dimensions
A	Side	2	¾" plywood	16" x 17"
B	Front	1	¾" plywood	16" x 41"
C	Support	8	2 x 2 pine	16" long
D	Leg	4	4 x 4 pine	44" long
E	Shelf Trim	2	2 x 4 pine	41" long
F	Short Brace	2	1 x 2 pine	15½"
G	Long Brace	2	1 x 2 pine	41" long
H	Shelf	1	¾" plywood	44" x 20"
I	Top	1	¾" plywood	24" x 48"
J	Front Trim	1	2 x 4 pine	51⅛"
K	Side Trim	2	2 x 4 pine	25¼" long
L	Front Lattice	1	Lattice	16" x 41"
M	Side Lattice	2	Lattice	16" x 17"
N	Rail Support	1	2 x 4 pine	52" long
O	Foot Rail	1	4"-wide top rail	52" long

Building the Frame

1. Cut two Sides (A) from ¾-inch-thick plywood, each measuring 16 x 17 inches.

2. Cut one Front (B) from ¾-inch-thick plywood, measuring 16 x 41 inches.

3. Cut eight Supports (C) from 2 x 2 pine, each measuring 16 inches long.

4. Place two Supports (C) on a level surface parallel to each other and 14 inches apart. Place the short end of one Side (A) over the Supports (C), as shown in figure 1. Apply glue to the meeting surfaces, and screw through the Side (A) into the Supports (C), using four 1⅝-inch wood screws in each Support (C).

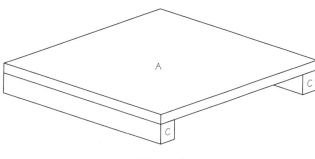

Figure 1

5. Repeat step 4 to assemble the remaining Side (A) and two Supports (C).

6. Place two Supports (C) parallel to each other on a level surface and 38 inches apart. In the same way that the Sides (A) were assembled, place the short end of the Front (B) over the two Supports (C). Apply glue to the meeting surfaces, and screw through the Front (B) into the Supports (C), using four 1⅝-inch screws in each Support (C).

Attaching the Posts

1. Cut four Legs (D) from 4 x 4 pine, each measuring 44 inches.

2. Place the assembled Front (B) and Supports (C) on edge and place one Leg (D) over the end of the Front (B) and Support (C) assembly, as shown in figure 2. Apply glue to the meeting surface, and clamp in place while you screw through the Support (C) into the Leg (D), using four 2½-inch wood screws.

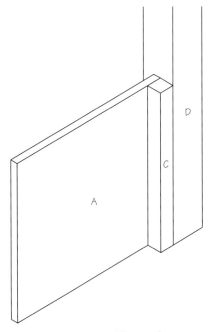

Figure 2

3. Repeat step 1 to attach a Leg (D) to the other end of the assembled Front (B).

4. Place one of the assembled Sides (A) on edge, place one Leg (D) over one end of the Front (B) and Support (C) assembly, as shown in figure 2. Apply glue to the meeting surface, and clamp in place while you screw through the Support (C) into the Leg (D), using four 2½-inch wood screws.

5. Repeat step 3 to attach another Leg (D) to the other end of the assembled Side (A).

6. Repeat steps 3 and 4 to attach the Legs (D) to the remaining Side (A).

7. Cut two Shelf Trims (E) from 2 x 4 pine, each measuring 41 inches.

8. Place the remaining two Supports (C) flat on a level surface parallel to each other and 41 inches apart. Place the two Shelf Trims (E) over the Supports (C), as shown in figure 3. Screw through the Shelf Trims (E) into the Supports (C), using two 2-inch wood screws per joint.

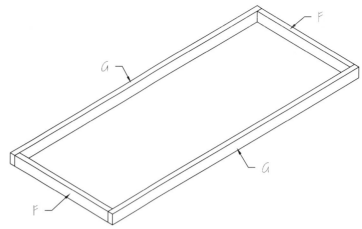

Figure 4

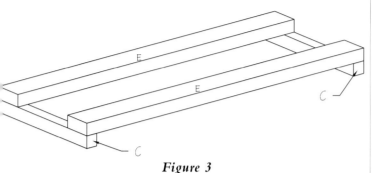

Figure 3

9. Place the assembled Shelf Trims (E) and Supports (C) between the Legs (D) of the assembled Sides (A) and parallel to the Front (A). Apply glue to the meeting surfaces, and screw through the Supports (C) into the Legs (D), using four 2-inch wood screws. Note: Make sure that the Shelf Trims (E) are facing away from the inside of the frame.

Adding the Shelf

1. Cut two Short Braces (F) from 1 x 2 pine, each measuring 15½ inches.

2. Cut two Long Braces (G) from 1 x 2 pine, each measuring 41 inches.

3. Position the two Short Braces (F) on edge, parallel to each other and 39½ inches apart.

4. Position the two Long Braces (G) over the ends of the Short Braces (F), as shown in figure 4. Apply glue to the meeting surfaces, and nail through the Long Braces (G) into the ends of the Short Braces (F), using two 2-inch finish nails in each joint.

5. Cut one Shelf (H) from ¾-inch-thick plywood, measuring 44 x 20 inches. Refer to figure 5 to cut out the corners.

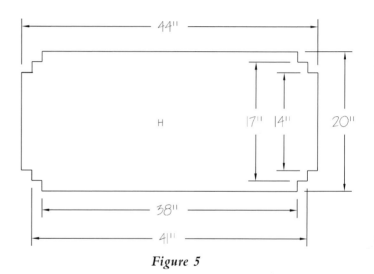

Figure 5

6. Place the Shelf (H) over the Long and Short Braces (F and G). Apply glue to the meeting surfaces, and nail through the Shelf (H) into the Short and Long Braces (F and G), using 1¼-inch finish nails spaced about every 5 inches.

7. The assembled shelf will be installed with the bar frame lying down and the Front (B) facing the work surface. Place the assembled shelf inside the four corners formed by the Supports (C), as shown in figure 6 (page 92). (Shelf not included in figure to better show braces.) Screw through the face of the Long and Short Braces (F and G) into the two Supports (C) in each corner, using 2-inch wood screws.

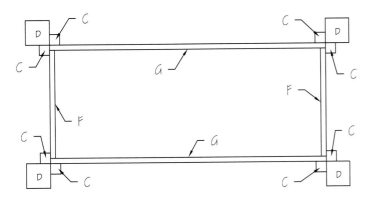

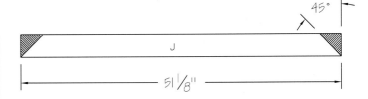

Figure 8

Figure 6

Adding the Top

1. Cut one Top (I) from ¾-inch-thick plywood, measuring 24 x 48 inches.

2. Turn the assembled bar over onto its legs. Place the Top (I) over the ends of the legs (D), as shown in figure 7. Screw through the Top (I) into the ends of the Legs (D), using two 2-inch wood screws in each corner.

4. Cut two Side Trims (K) from 2 x 4 pine, each measuring 25¼ inches. We beveled one edge as we did for the front trim pieces and mitered one end of each board. Note: The miters on each board are opposites of each other.

5. Attach the Front Trim (J) to the Legs (D) and Top (I), keeping the beveled edge of the Front Trim (J) up and ¼ inch above the Top (I) to leave room for the tile to be installed. Screw through the Front Trim (J) into the Legs (D), using two 2½-inch wood screws in each Leg (D).

6. Attach one Side Trim (K) to one side of the bar, so that the 45° miters meet. Screw through the Side Trim (K) into the Legs (D), using two 2-½-inch screws in each leg.

7. Repeat step 6 to attach the remaining Side Trim (K).

Adding the Lattice and Foot Rail

1. Cut one Front Lattice (L) from lattice, measuring 16 x 41 inches.

2. Place the Front Lattice (L) over the Front (B). Apply glue to the meeting surfaces, and nail through the Front Lattice (L), using 1-inch finish nails.

3. Cut two Side Lattices (M) from lattice, each measuring 16 x 17 inches.

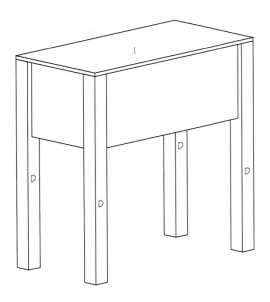

Figure 7

3. Cut one Front Trim (J) from 2 x 4 pine, measuring 51⅛ inches. An optional step at this point is to bevel the edge of the trim at a 30° angle. The corners are also mitered at opposing 45° angles, as shown in figure 8.

4. Place one Side Lattice (M) over one Side (A). Apply glue to the meeting surfaces, and nail through the Side Lattice (M), using 1-inch finish nails.

5. Repeat step 4 to attach the remaining Side Lattice (M) to the opposite Side (A).

6. Cut one Rail Support (N) from 2 x 4 pine, measuring 52 inches.

7. Bevel one edge of the Rail Support (N) at a 45° angle along its length.

8. Center the Rail Support (N) over the two front Legs (D), 8 inches from the ground. Note that the Rail Support (N) will extend past the Legs (D) about 2 inches on each side. Apply glue to the meeting surfaces, and screw through the Rail Support (N) into the Legs (D), using two 2-inch wood screws on each joint.

9. Cut one Foot Rail (O) from 4-inch-wide top rail, measuring 52 inches.

10. Place the Foot Rail (O) over the Rail Support (N). Apply glue to the meeting surfaces, and screw through the Foot Rail (O) into the Rail Support (N), using 2-inch wood screws spaced every 6 inches.

Adding the Tile

1. Following the manufacturer's directions, carefully spread an even coat of the tile adhesive over the surface of the Top (I) with an ⅛-inch V trowel.

2. Place the tiles on the adhesive one at a time, making sure that they are positioned correctly. Do not slide the tiles, or the adhesive will be forced up on the sides of the tile. Let the adhesive dry overnight.

3. Mix the tile grout according to the manufacturer's directions.

4. Spread the grout over the tile, using a rubber-surfaced float held at a 45° angle so that the grout is forced evenly into the spaces between the tiles.

5. Use a wet sponge to wipe the excess grout off the

tiles and joints; if you let it dry, the hardened grout will be very difficult to remove. Try to use as little water as possible when removing the excess, so that you do not thin the grout that remains. Let the grout dry overnight.

6. Rinse the remaining film from the tile and wipe it dry with an old towel.

7. Apply grout sealer, following the manufacturer's directions.

Finishing

1. Sand the entire bar thoroughly.

2. Finish with a stain (we used cherry stain and green paint for the trim on this one), or leave natural.

Cocktail Table With Tray

This cocktail table does double duty—as a handy side table as well as a removable tabletop serving tray. It is the perfect size for carrying plates, pitchers, glasses, and many other items from the kitchen.

33 linear feet of 1 x 4 pine

6 linear feet of 1 x 1 pine

7 linear feet of 1 x 6 pine

Scrap wood

Hardware

120 1¼" wood screws

10 2½" wood screws

20 1⅜" wood screws

Special Tools and Techniques

Miter

Cutting List

Code	Description	Qty.	Materials	Dimensions
A	Side Connector	2	1 x 4 pine	15½" long
B	Leg	8	1 x 4 pine	16" long
C	Side Spacer	2	1 x 4 pine	15½" long
D	Front/Back Connector	2	1 x 4 pine	14" long
E	Front/Back Spacer	2	1 x 4 pine	8½" long
F	Leg Support	4	1 x 1 pine	16" long
G	Corner Support	4	1 x 4 pine	8½" long
H	Top Slat	3	1 x 6 pine	20" long
I	Long Tray Side	2	1 x 4 pine	22" long
J	Short Tray Side	2	1 x 4 pine	17½" long
K	Narrow Tray Slat	3	1 x 4 pine	20½" long
L	Wide Tray Slat	1	1 x 6 pine	20½" long

Constructing the Side Assemblies

1. The table consists of two side assemblies: a front assembly and a back assembly. The construction of these assemblies is shown in figure 2 (page 96).

2. To make the side assemblies, cut two Side Connectors (A) from 1 x 4 pine, each measuring 15½ inches.

3. Cut four Legs (B) from 1 x 4 pine, each measuring 16 inches.

4. Position one Side Connector (A) over two Legs (B), spacing the pieces as shown in figure 1 (page 96). The upper end of the Side Connector (A) should be flush with the ends of the Legs (B), and there should be a ¾-inch offset at each end of the Side Connector (A). Apply glue to the meeting surfaces, and screw through the Side Connector (A) into the Legs (B), using two 1¼-inch wood screws on each joint.

5. Cut two Side Spacers (C) from 1 x 4 pine, each measuring 15½ inches.

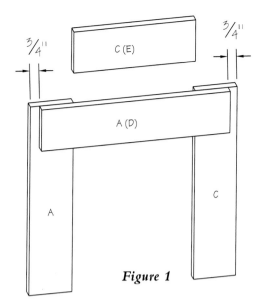

Figure 1

6. Place one Side Spacer (C) between the two legs (B), as shown in figure 1. Apply glue to the meeting surfaces, and screw through the Side Connector (A) into the Side Spacer (C), using three evenly spaced 1¼-inch wood screws.

7. Repeat steps 1 through 6 to construct a second side assembly, using the remaining two Legs (B) and the remaining Side Connector (A) and Side Spacer (C).

Constructing the Front and Back Assemblies

1. The front and back assemblies are constructed in the same fashion as the side assemblies (see figure 1). Cut four Legs (B) from 1 x 4 pine, each measuring 16 inches.

2. Cut two Front/Back Connectors (D) from 1 x 4 pine, each measuring 14 inches.

3. Assemble two Legs (B) and one Front/Back Connector (D), spacing the parts as shown in figure 1. Again, the pieces should be flush at the top, and there should be a ¾-inch offset at the ends of the Front/Back Connector (D). Secure the joints with glue and two 1¼-inch wood screws.

4. Cut two Front/Back Spacers (E) from 1 x 4 pine, each measuring 8½ inches.

5. Insert one Front/Back Spacer (E) between the two Legs (B). Apply glue to the meeting surfaces, and screw through the Front/Back Connector (D) into the Front/Back Spacer (E), using three evenly spaced 1¼-inch wood screws.

6. Repeat steps 1 through 5 to construct a back assembly identical to the front assembly, using the remaining two Legs (B), as well as the remaining Front/Back Connector (D) and Front/Back Spacer (E).

Joining the Assemblies

1. Attach the two side assemblies to the front and back assemblies as shown in figure 2, making certain that the Legs (B) are flush at both the top and the bottom. Note that the front and back assemblies overlap the exposed ends of the side assemblies. When properly assembled, the outside of the table should measure 15½ x 18½ inches. Apply glue to the meeting surfaces, and screw through the

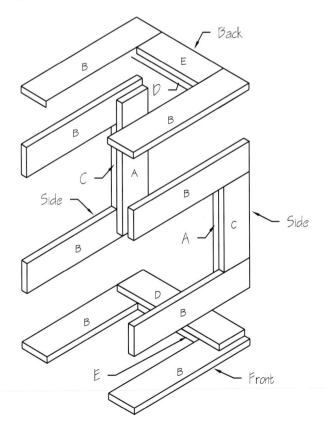

Figure 2

overlapping Legs (B) into the adjoining Legs (B), using 1¼-inch wood screws spaced about every 5 inches.

2. Cut four Leg Supports (F) from 1 x 1 pine, each measuring 16 inches.

3. Apply glue to the meeting surfaces, and attach one Leg Support (F) to the inside corner of each of the four leg assemblies, as shown in figure 3. Screw through the Leg Supports (F) into each of the Legs (B), using four evenly spaced 1¼-inch wood screws.

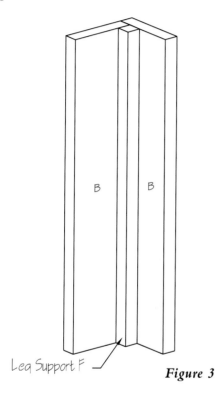

Figure 3

4. Cut four Corner Supports (G) from 1 x 4 pine, each measuring 8½ inches.

5. Set each Corner Support (G) on its face, and miter the ends at opposing 45° angles, as shown in figure 4.

6. Using figure 5 as a guide, position the mitered Corner Supports (G), making sure that their faces are flush with the top edges of the assembled frame. Apply glue to the meeting surfaces, and screw at an angle through the edges of each of the Corner Supports (G) into the frame assembly, using a 2½-inch wood screw on each joint.

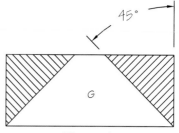

Figure 4

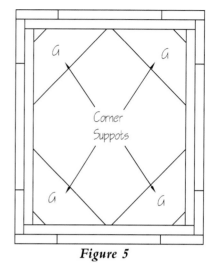

Figure 5

Adding the Top

1. Cut three Top Slats (H) from 1 x 6 pine, each measuring 20 inches.

2. Place the three Top Slats (H) over the top of the assembly, spacing them evenly so that the tabletop measures 17 inches wide and 20 inches long, and the tabletop extends ¾ inch over the sides, back, and front of the assembly, as shown in figure 6.

3. Apply glue to the meeting surfaces, and screw through the Top Slats (H) into the Corner

Figure 6

Supports (G) and the frame assembly, using 1¼-inch wood screws.

Making the Table Tray

1. Cut two Long Tray Sides (I) from 1 x 4 pine, each measuring 22 inches.

2. Cut two Short Tray Sides (J) from 1 x 4 pine, each measuring 17½ inches.

3. Position the two Long Tray Sides (I) on edge, parallel to each other and 17½ inches apart. Fit the two Short Tray Sides (J) between the ends of the Long Tray Sides (I), as shown in figure 7. Apply glue to the meeting surfaces, and screw through the Long Tray Sides (I) into the ends of the Short Tray Sides (J), using two 1⅝-inch wood screws on each joint.

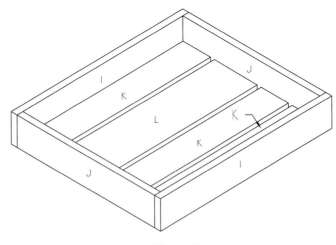

Figure 8

Finishing

1. Fill the cracks, crevices, and screw holes with wood filler.

2. Sand the completed tray and table thoroughly.

3. Stain or paint the table and tray the color(s) of your choice, or leave the natural color and seal with a waterproof sealer.

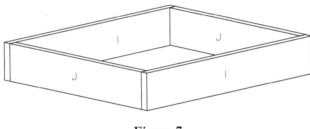

Figure 7

4. Cut three Narrow Tray Slats (K) from 1 x 4 pine, each measuring 20½ inches.

5. Cut one Wide Tray Slat (L) from 1 x 6 pine, measuring 20½ inches.

6. Place the assembled tray sides (I and J) on a flat surface. In order to elevate the Narrow and Wide Tray Slats (K and L), place several pieces of 1-inch-thick scrap wood inside the assembly. Then place the four Slats (K and L) inside the assembly, as shown in figure 8, spacing them evenly over the bottom. Apply glue to the meeting surfaces, and screw through the Short Tray Sides (J) into the Slats (K and L), using two 1⅝-inch screws on each joint.

Hurricane Lamp

Add a little romance to your backyard with a hurricane lamp. This simple project solves the problem of keeping candles lit out-of-doors. Constructed of one sturdy shelf and two ornamental gingerbread shelf brackets, it holds a hurricane globe and a generous-sized candle.

Materials (for one lamp)

1 linear foot of 2 x 8 pine

5 linear feet of 1 x 1 pine

Glass hurricane globe, measuring just less than 5"
   in diameter and 11½" high★

Hardware

20 1⅝" finish nails

Premade ornamental shelf brackets, 5" x 8"

*Notes on Materials and Hardware

Any size glass hurricane globe up to 5 inches in diameter will work for this project, but the dimensions of the Front/Backs (B) and the Sides (C) will have to be altered to accommodate a smaller size. The premade ornamental shelf brackets are available at most hardware and building supply stores. They already have a metal hanger installed in the back and come in a variety of designs.

Cutting List

Code	Description	Qty.	Materials	Dimensions
A	Base	1	2 x 8 pine	10" long
B	Front/Back	2	1 x 1 pine	5" long
C	Sides	2	1 x 1 pine	6½" long

Cutting the Pieces

1. Cut one Base (A) from 2 x 8 pine, measuring 10 inches.

2. Cut two Back/Fronts (B) from 1 x 1 pine, each measuring 5 inches.

3. Cut two Sides (C) from 1 x 1 pine, each measuring 6½ inches.

Assembling the Lamp

1. Place the Base (A) on a level surface. Position one Back/Front (B) lengthwise against one edge of the Base (A), 2½ inches from each end, as shown in figure 1. Apply glue to the meeting surfaces, and nail through the Back/Front (B) into the Base (A), using two 1⅝-inch finish nails.

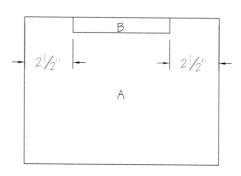

Figure 1

2. Repeat step 1 to attach the second Front/Back (A) to the base, parallel to and 5 inches from the first, as shown in figure 2 (page 102).

3. Place the Sides (C) over the ends of the Front/Backs (A), to form a 6½-inch square (outside measurement), as shown in figure 2 (page 102). Apply glue to the meeting surfaces, and nail through the Sides (C) into the Base (A), using two 1⅝-inch finish nails on each piece.

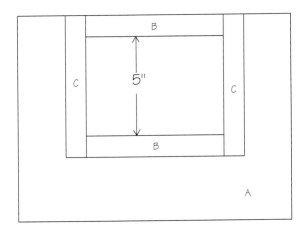

Figure 2

4. Turn the base assembly upside down, and attach the 6-inch edge of the ornamental shelf brackets to each end of the Base (A) so that the back of the bracket, which has a metal hanger, is flush with the back of the base assembly. Apply glue to the meeting surfaces, and nail through the sides of the ornamental shelf brackets into the Base (A), using six 1⅝-inch finish nails on each bracket.

Finishing

1. Fill any cracks, crevices, and nail holes with wood filler, and sand the lamp thoroughly.

2. Paint or stain the lamp the color of your choice—we chose seafoam green.

3. Hang the completed base on your wall or fence, utilizing the metal hangers on the back of the shelf bracket.

4. Install the candle and glass hurricane globe.

Coffee Table

Every outdoor living area needs a coffee table, and we are very proud of this one. It has a tiled center section, so it is easy to clean up and always looks nice. The table legs are adorned with fence-post finials, making the table seem a more complicated project than it actually is.

*Notes on Materials

The wooden finials we used for the table "feet" are designed to be used on a fence post. They can be purchased at most building-supply stores and have a large screw already attached in the center. The ones we used are 3 inches tall. You can substitute any exterior-rated finial you like, but if it is taller than 3 inches, be sure to adjust the length of your table legs accordingly, or your completed coffee table will not be the correct height.

When choosing tile for this table, consider that you must cover an area measuring 3½ square feet. We used standard 4-inch-square tiles. If the tile you purchased does not fit within these dimensions, you can either alter the dimensions of the table or cut some of the tiles to fit, using a tile cutter. Tile cutters can be rented at home centers and hardware stores, or some home centers will cut them for you.

Materials

16 linear feet of 1 x 4 pine

2' x 4' sheet of ¾" plywood★

6 linear feet of 4 x 4 pine

4 fence-post finials, approximately 3" high and
    3½" in diameter★

32 4"-square tiles, or your choice of any tile
    that covers an area measuring 3½ sq. feet

Waterproof tile adhesive

5 lbs. tile grout

Small bottle of grout sealer

Hardware

25 1¼" (3d) finish nails

35 1⅝-inch wood screws

10 2½-inch wood screws

Special Tools and Techniques

Framing or speed square

Tile cutter (optional)

⅛" V trowel

Rubber tile float

Cutting List

Code	Description	Qty.	Materials	Dimensions
A	Long Trim	2	1 x 4 pine	39-½" long
B	Short Trim	2	1 x 4 pine	16-½" long
C	Top	1	¾" plywood	19-½" x 35-½"
D	Long Side	2	1 x 4 pine	35-½" long
E	Short Side	2	1 x 4 pine	21" long
F	Leg	4	4 x 4 pine	13" long

Making the Tabletop

1. Cut two Long Trims (A) from 1 x 4 pine, each measuring 39½ inches.

2. Cut two Short Trims (B) from 1 x 4 pine, each measuring 16½ inches.

3. Cut one Top (C) from ¾-inch plywood, measuring 19½ x 35½ inches.

4. Place the Long Trims (A) flat on the work surface, parallel to each other and 16¼ inches apart.

5. Position the Short Trims (B) between the Long Trims (A), then place the Top (C) over the Short and Long Trims (A and B), as shown in figure 1. When the Top (C) is perfectly centered, the Short and Long Trims (A and B) should extend beyond the Top (C) by 2 inches on all sides. Apply glue to the meeting surfaces, and nail through the Top (C) into the Long and Short Trims (A and B), using 1¼-inch finish nails every 6 inches.

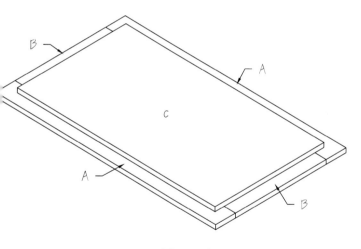

Figure 1

Making the Base

1. Cut two Long Sides (D) from 1 x 4 pine, each measuring 35½ inches.

2. Cut two Short Sides (E) from 1 x 4 pine, each measuring 21 inches.

3. Place the two Long Sides (D) on edge, parallel to

each other and 19½ inches apart. Fit the two Short Sides (E) over the ends of the two Long Sides (D) to form a rectangle measuring 21 x 37 inches. (See figure 2.) Apply glue to the meeting surfaces, and screw through the Short Sides (E) into the ends of the Long Sides (D), using two 1⅝-inch wood screws on each joint.

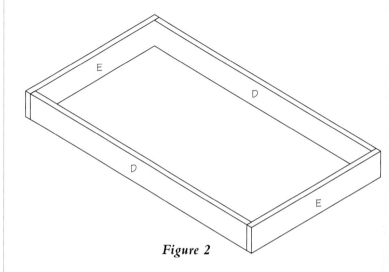

Figure 2

4. Place the assembled Long and Short Sides (D and E) over the Top (C) so that the assembled Long and Short Sides (D and E) fit around the plywood as shown in figure 3. Apply glue to the meeting surfaces, and screw through the Long and Short Sides (D and E) into the plywood Top (C) every 6 inches, using 1⅝-inch wood screws

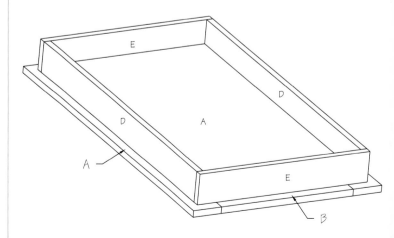

Figure 3

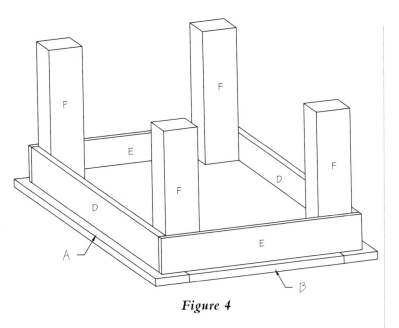

Figure 4

Attaching the Legs

1. Cut four Legs (F) from 4 x 4 pine, each measuring 13 inches.

2. Place the four Legs (F) at the four corners of the assembled Top (C), as shown in figure 4. Use a square to make sure the Legs (F) are straight so that the table is not crooked when turned right side up. Apply glue to the meeting surfaces, and screw through the Long and Short Sides (D and E) into the Legs (F), using 2½-inch wood screws (4 screws in each leg, and 2 screws in each side).

3. To attach the fence-post finials to the exposed ends of the four Legs (F), predrill a starter hole in the center of each Leg (F). Screw a fence-post finial into each Leg (F).

Adding the Tile

1. Following the manufacturer's directions, carefully spread an even coat of the tile adhesive over the surface of the Top (C) with an ⅛-inch V trowel.

2. Place the tiles on the adhesive one at a time, making sure that they are positioned correctly. Do not slide the tiles, or the adhesive will be forced up on the sides of the tile. Let the adhesive dry overnight.

3. Mix the tile grout according to the manufacturer's directions.

4. Spread the grout over the tile using a rubber-surfaced float held at a 45° angle so that the grout is forced evenly into the spaces between the tiles.

5. Use a wet sponge to wipe the excess grout off the tiles and joints; if you let this excess grout dry, the hardened grout will be very difficult to remove. Try to use as little water as possible when removing the excess, so that you do not thin the grout that remains. Let the grout dry overnight.

6. Rinse the remaining film from the tile and wipe it with an old towel.

7. Apply grout sealer, following the manufacturer's directions.

Finishing

1. Fill any cracks or crevices with wood filler, and thoroughly sand all surfaces of the completed table.

2. Either paint or stain the wood portions of the coffee table the color of your choice, or simply leave it natural.

Mini Gazebo

Since a traditional gazebo has eight sides and this one has four, Mark suggested that the proper name for this project should be either a "Gaz" or an "Ebo." Whatever you call it, it is a pretty addition to any yard, and provides a quiet nook for reading, drinking lemonade, or just enjoying the day. The gazebo is easy to build if you take it one step at a time. It is built in sections from the ground up, beginning with the bottom frame.

Materials

- 32 linear feet of 2 x 6 pine
- 4 8' 4 x 4 pine posts
- 4 concrete footings
- 1 package shims
- 90 linear feet of 5/4 x 6 pine decking
- 34 linear feet of 2 x 4 pine
- 4' x 4' sheet of 1/4" plywood
- 4 4' x 8' sheets of 1/2" plywood
- Shingles, enough to cover 75 square feet
- 14 linear feet of 1 x 4 pine
- 58 linear feet of 1 x 1 pine
- 3, 4' x 8' sheets of lattice

Hardware

- 100 3½" wood screws
- 16 3½" lag screws
- 120 2½" wood screws
- 220 1⅝" wood screws
- 70 2" wood screws
- 500 1" roofing nails
- 50 2" (6d) finish nails
- 300 1¼" (3d) finish nails

Special Tools and Techniques

- Miter
- Level

Cutting List

Code	Description	Qty.	Materials	Dimensions
A	Front/Back	2	2 x 6 pine	57½" long
B	Sides	2	2 x 6 pine	60½" long
C	Center Support	1	2 x 6 pine	57½" long
D	Corner Post	4	4 x 4 pine posts	96" long
E	Floorboards	11	5/4 x 6 pine	60½" long
F	Roof Supports	2	2 x 4 pine	85" long
G	Roof Rafter	2	2 x 4 pine	59" long
H	Rafter Connector	2	1/4" plywood	see figure
I	Rafter Brace	2	2 x 4 pine	58" long
J	Roof	4	1/2" plywood	47" x 74"
K	Peak Cover Sides	4	2 x 6 pine	16" long
L	Planter Outer Side	3	5/4 x 6 pine	58¾" long
M	Planter Inner Side	2	5/4 x 6 pine	54" long
N	Planter Middle	1	5/4 x 6 pine	49¾" long
O	Planter End	2	5/4 x 6 pine	5½" long
P	Planter Bottom	3	1 x 4 pine	49½" long
Q	Vertical Support	12	1 x 1 pine	32" long
R	Horizontal Support	6	1 x 1 pine	48" long
S	Trellis Panel	3	lattice	32" x 49½"

Building the Bottom Frame

1. Cut two Back/Fronts (A) from 2 x 6 pine, each measuring 57½ inches.

2. Cut two Sides (B) from 2 x 6 pine, each measuring 60½ inches.

3. Position the two Back/Fronts (A) on a level surface, parallel to each other and 57½ inches apart.

4. Place one Side (B) against the ends of the two Back/Fronts (A) to form a 60½-inch square, as shown in figure 1. Screw through the ends of the Side (B) into the Back/Fronts (A), using two 3½-inch wood screws on each joint.

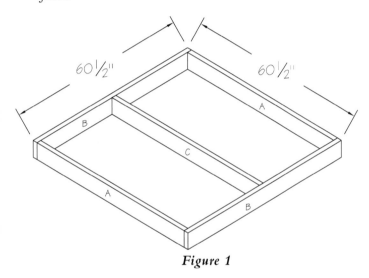

Figure 1

5. Cut one Center Support (C) from 2 x 6 pine, measuring 57½ inches long.

6. Place the Center Support (C) between the two Front/Backs (A), centered between the Sides (B) inside the bottom frame, as shown in figure 1. Screw through the two Front/Backs (A) into the ends of the Center Support (C), using three 3½-inch wood screws on each joint.

Adding the Posts

1. Place four concrete footings on the ground to form a square. The distance between the four outer corners of the post openings in the concrete footings should measure exactly 57½ inches, as shown in figure 2. When the footings are exactly square, the measurement between opposing corners should be exactly the same.

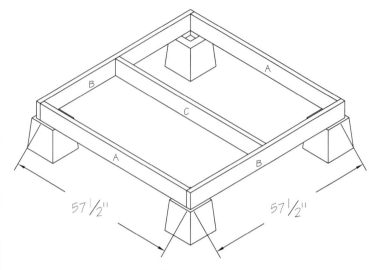

Figure 2

2. Place the assembled bottom frame over the concrete footings, as shown in figure 2. To level the bottom frame, it is a good idea to enlist the assistance of a helper. Beginning at the highest corner, level each of the remaining three corners, working in rotation around the bottom frame. Use shims to level the frame. Insert the thin end of the shim underneath the Corner Post (D) until that edge of the Corner Post (D) is level.

3. Cut about 1 inch off the end of the four Corner Posts (D) so that one end of each Corner Post (D) is square.

4. When you are satisfied that the bottom frame is exactly level and square, insert a Corner Post (D) inside the bottom frame (squared end down) on one corner of the structure. Use a level vertically to make certain that the Corner Post (D) is plumb. Temporarily hold the post in place by screwing through the bottom frame into the Corner Post (D), using two 3½-inch wood screws (one on each side of the post).

5. Repeat steps 3 and 4 three times to add the remaining three Corner Posts (D) to the structure.

6. Recheck the level and squareness of the structure, and when it is perfect, predrill holes and insert a 3½-inch lag screw through the bottom frame into the each side of each Corner Post (D).

Adding the Floorboards

1. Cut 11 Floorboards (E) from ¾ x 6 decking, each measuring 60½ inches.

2. Since the Floorboards (E) must be cut to fit around the Corner Posts (D), follow the cutout measurements and the placement sequence, as shown in figure 3 to add the Floorboards (E) to the structure. Cut and place one Floorboard (E) at a time, beginning with number 1 and ending with number 11. Because of variations in lumber sizes, it may be necessary to retrim some of the Floorboards (E). Make certain that each of your Floorboards (E) fits correctly before cutting the next one. The Floorboards (E) will overhang the Front/Back (A) and Sides (B) by 1¾ inches. Screw through each Floorboard (E) into the Sides (B) and Center Support (C), using two 2½-inch wood screws on each joint.

Adding the Top Frame

1. Repeat the section Building the Bottom Frame (steps 1 through 5) to assemble a top frame that is identical to the bottom frame. To make certain that the top and bottom frames are identical, we suggest that you assemble the top frame around the existing posts on top of the Floorboards (E).

2. You will need a trusty helper for this step. Mark the desired height of the lower edge of the top frame on each of the four Corner Posts (D). We attached ours 6½ feet above the Floorboards (E). Raise the top frame to the height desired, and make certain it is level on all four sides. We used an extra board to prop the top frame in place until we had it leveled and could secure it.

3. When you are satisfied that the top frame and all four Corner Posts (D) are exactly level and square, hold the assembly in place temporarily by screwing through the Front/Backs (A) and Sides (B) into the Corner Post (D), using one 3½-inch wood screw. To hold it securely, predrill holes and insert one 3½-inch lag screw through each Front/Back (A) and Side (B) into the each Corner Post (D).

4. Cut off the top of each of the Corner Posts (D) flush with the upper edge of the top frame.

Adding the Rafters

1. Cut two Roof Supports (F) from 2 x 4 pine, each measuring 85 inches.

2. Miter each end of both Roof Supports (F) at opposing 60° angles, as shown in figure 4.

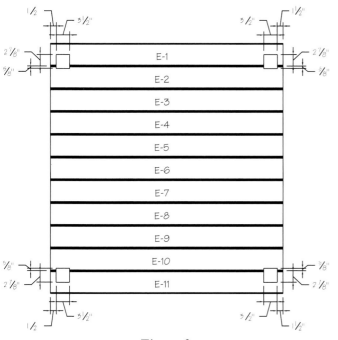

Figure 3

Figure 4

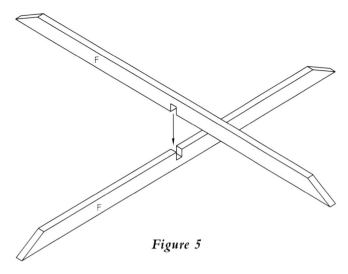

Figure 5

3. The two Roof Supports (F) fit together by means of a slot system (see figure 5). Cut a notch measuring 1½ inches wide and 1¾ inches deep in the exact center of both Roof Supports (F). Make certain that you make these cuts very carefully (watching the direction of your mitered ends), or the Roof Supports (F) will not fit together correctly. The two Roof Supports (F) will be joined in a later step.

4. Cut two Roof Rafters (G) from 2 x 4 pine, each measuring 59 inches.

5. Miter one end of each Roof Rafter (G) at a 30° angle, as shown in figure 6.

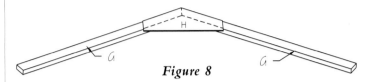

Figure 6

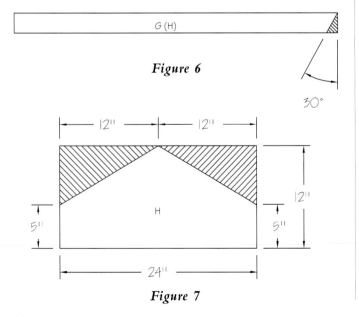

Figure 7

6. Cut two Rafter Connectors (H) from ¼-inch plywood, following the measurements given in figure 7.

7. Place two Roof Rafters (G), mitered ends together, on a level surface. Place one Rafter Connector (H) over the mitered joint, as shown in figure 8. Apply glue to the

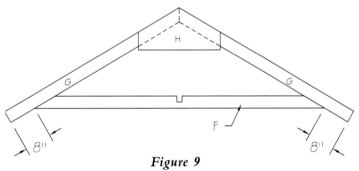

Figure 8

meeting surfaces, and screw through the Rafter Connector (H) into both Roof Rafters (G), using 1⅝-inch wood screws spaced every 3 inches.

8. Turn the assembly over and attach the remaining Rafter Connector (H) to the opposite side of the two Roof Rafters (G).

9. Fit the Roof Support (F) between the ends of the Roof Rafters (G), as shown in figure 9. Apply glue to the

Figure 9

meeting surfaces, and screw through the ends of the Roof Support (F) into the Roof Rafters (G), using two 3½-inch wood screws on each joint.

10. Apply glue to the inner edges of the notches, then fit the slots in the two Roof Supports (F) together so that the Roof Supports (F) form an X shape as shown in figure 10. Screw through the top Roof Support (F) into the notch, using a 2-inch wood screw.

11. Cut two Rafter Braces (I) from 2 x 4 pine, each measuring 58 inches.

12. Miter one end of each Rafter Brace (I) at a 30° angle, as shown in figure 6.

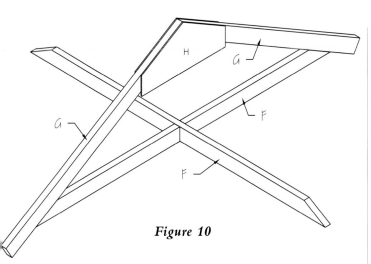

Figure 10

13. Install the Rafter Braces (I), mitered end against the Rafter Connector (H) and perpendicular to the Roof Rafters (G), as shown in figure 11. Screw through the Rafter Braces (I) and the Rafter Connector (H) and into the Roof Rafters (G), using two 3½-inch wood screws. Attach the other end of the Rafter Braces (I) to the free ends of the Roof Supports (F). Screw through the Roof

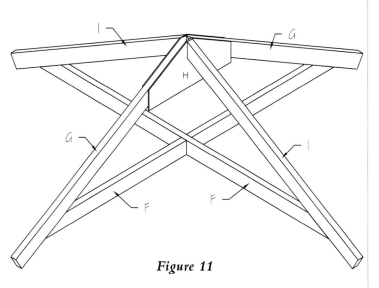

Figure 11

Supports (F) into the Rafter Braces (I), using two 2½-inch wood screws.

14. Now it is time for the scaffolding. Place the entire roof support structure on top of the posts and top frame. The Roof Supports (F) should be centered over each of the four corner posts. Screw at an angle through the Roof Supports (F) into the Corner Post (D), using one 3½-inch wood screw on each side of the Roof Support (F). If you

are building this project in an area that receives high winds, we suggest that you add metal straps over each of the Roof Support (F).

Adding the Roof

1. Cut four Roofs (J) from ½-inch-thick plywood, following the dimensions given in figure 12.

2. Place each of the Roofs (J) over the roof support assembly, working in rotation around the structure. Screw through the edges of each of the Roofs (J), using 1⅝-inch wood screws spaced every 5 inches. (This roof assembly does not have to look perfect, as it will be covered with shingles.)

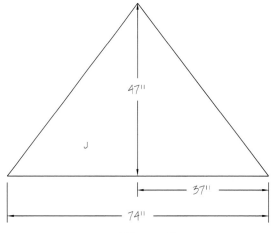

Figure 12

Adding the Shingles

1. We used six rows of shingles to cover each side of the gazebo. On the top two rows, we trimmed regular-size shingles to the appropriate length, so they did not extend past the roof peak. It is better to work with the top portion of the original shingle, since it is thinner than the bottom edge. It is not difficult to shingle, and since the finished project should look somewhat rustic, this job is even easier. Begin attaching the first row of shingles with 1-inch roofing nails, just overlapping the bottom edge of one Roof (J). Each shingle should be nailed twice to prevent shifting. Choose random widths of shingles as you work. Continue the row across the bottom edge.

2. Next, add a second row, overlapping the first row by about 6 inches higher. Continue adding rows, about 6 inches apart, until you reach the roof peak. It is helpful to mark each row with a pencil, using a long level to keep your rows level and straight.

3. Trim off the shingle excess on each side and on the peak. Repeat the application of shingles on the remaining three Roofs (J). The row placement on each Roof (J) should match the height of the ones on the first Roof (J).

4. To cover the roof ridges, cut the shingles to 2 inches wide, and attach the resulting narrow shingles to both sides of each of the four roof ridges, working from the bottom up. Trim the last shingles, so they do not extend past the roof ridges or peak.

Adding the Peak Cover

1. Cut four Peak Cover Sides (K) from 2 x 6 pine, each measuring 16 inches.

2. Miter each end of the four Peak Cover Sides (K) at opposing 45° angles, as shown in figure 13.

3. Position two Peak Cover Sides (K) on a level surface, parallel to each other and 13 inches apart, with miters

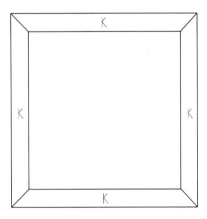

Figure 13

facing each other. Fit the remaining two Peak Cover Sides (K) between the first two, matching miters, to form a 16-inch square. Apply glue to the meeting surfaces, and screw through each side of all four corners, using two 2½-inch wood screws on each joint.

4. Place the assembled peak cover over the roof peak. Center and level the peak cover on all four sides. Secure the peak cover to the roof by screwing at an angle through the peak cover into the roof, at least once on each of the four sides of the roof, using 3½-inch wood screws.

Adding the Planter Boxes

1. Cut three Planter Outer Sides (L), from ¾ x 6 deck boards, each measuring 58¾ inches.

2. Cut two Planter Inner Sides (M) from ¾ x 6 deck boards, each measuring 54 inches.

3. Cut one Planter Middle (N) from ¾ x 6 deck boards, measuring 49¾ inches.

4. Cut two Planter Ends (O) from ¾ x 6 deck boards, each measuring 5½ inches.

5. The planter boxes are built around the four Corner Posts (D). Measure and mark each of the four Corner Posts (D) at a height of 32 inches above the Floorboards (E). Each of the six planter pieces (L, M, N, and O) is mitered on both ends. The ends of the three Planter Outer Sides (L), Planter Middle (N), and Planter Ends (O) are mitered at opposing 45° angles. The two Planter Inner Sides (M) are mitered at the same 45° angle. Refer to figure 13 to be certain that your 45° miter is cut properly.

6. Measure your structure carefully and work in rotation around the Corner Posts (D). First add the three Planter Outer Sides (L), one at a time, then add one Planter Inner Side (M), then the Planter Middle (N), the remaining Inner Side (M), and finally the Planter Ends (O). Apply glue to the meeting surfaces, and use two 2½-inch wood screws on each joint.

7. Cut three Planter Bottoms (P) from 1 x 4 pine, each measuring 49½ inches.

8. Insert one Planter Bottom (P) flush with the bottom edge of the Outer and Inner Planter Sides (L and M). Nail through the Outer and Inner Planter Sides (L and M) into the edges of the Planter Bottom (P), using 2-inch finish nails spaced every 5 inches.

9. Repeat step 8 to add the remaining Planter Bottoms (P) to the opposite side and back of the structure.

Adding the Trellis

1. Cut 12 Vertical Supports (Q) from 1 x 1 pine, each measuring 32 inches.

2. Cut six Horizontal Supports (R) from 1 x 1 pine, each measuring 48 inches. Attach one of the Vertical Supports (Q) under the planter to the inside of one Corner Post (D), ¾ inch from the edge, as shown in figure 14. Apply glue to the meeting surfaces, and nail through the Vertical Support (Q) into the face of the Corner Post (D), using 1¼-inch finish nails spaced every 4 inches.

3. Repeat step 2 five times to attach the remaining Vertical Supports (Q) to the remaining three Corner Posts (D).

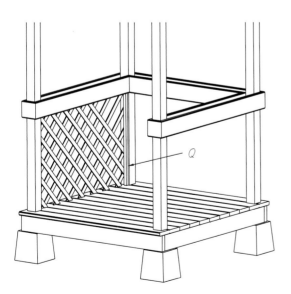

Figure 14

4. Attach one of the Horizontal Supports (R) to one Planter Bottom (P), between the two Vertical Supports (Q), again ¾ inch in from the edge. Apply glue to the meeting surfaces, and nail through the Horizontal Support (R) into the face of the Planter Bottom (P), using 1¼-inch finish nails spaced every 4 inches.

5. Repeat step 4 twice to attach the remaining Horizontal Supports (R) to the two remaining Planter Bottoms (P).

6. Cut three Trellis Panels (S) from lattice, each measuring 32 x 49½ inches.

7. Place one Trellis Panel (S) over the Horizontal and Vertical Supports (Q and R), as shown in figure 13.

8. Nail through the Trellis Panel (S) into the Horizontal and Vertical Supports (Q and R), using 1¼-inch finish nails spaced 6 inches apart.

9. Repeat step 8 twice to add the remaining two Trellis Panels (S) under the Planter Bottoms (P).

10. Repeat steps 3 through 6 to add one Horizontal and two Vertical Supports (Q and R) on the opposite side of each Trellis Panel (S). Horizontal supports have not been added to the bottom of the lattice, to make it easier to hose debris off the completed structure.

Finishing

1. We backfilled with extra dirt around our gazebo, then added sod over the dirt to hold it in place.

2. Sand off any rough edges on the structure.

3. Paint or stain the gazebo the color of your choice, or leave it the natural wood color.

Fence Planter Box

This project transforms a plain fence into a fabulous decorative element. It's quick to make, and, with the addition of some charming (albeit pre-made and readily available) ornamental gingerbread, it will certainly perk up any uninteresting space in your yard.

Materials

10 linear feet of 1 x 6 pine	
2 premade wooden gingerbread ornaments, approximately 6" x 8" inches each	

Hardware

50	1⅝" wood screws
20	1" (2d) finish nails
3	3½" wood screws (optional)

Cutting List

Code	Description	Qty.	Materials	Dimensions
A	Front/Back	2	1 x 6 pine	36" long
B	Side	2	1 x 6 pine	5½" long
C	Bottom	1	1 x 6 pine	34½" long

Making the Planter Box

1. Cut two Front/Backs (A) from 1 x 6 pine, each measuring 36 inches.

2. Cut two Sides (B) from 1 x 6 pine, each measuring 5½ inches.

3. Position the two Front/Backs (A) on a level surface, parallel to each other and 5½ inches apart. Fit the two Sides (B) between the two Front/Backs (A) to form a rectangle measuring 36 x 7 inches, as shown in figure 1.

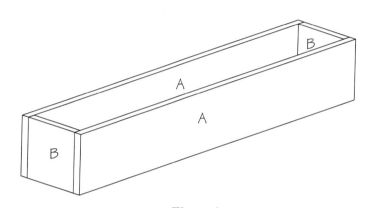

Figure 1

Apply glue to the meeting surfaces, and nail through the Front/Backs (A) into the Sides (B), using three evenly spaced 1⅝-inch screws on each joint.

4. Cut one Bottom (C) from 1 x 6 pine, measuring 34½ inches.

5. Insert the Bottom (C) inside the assembled rectangle, flush with the bottom edges of the Front/Backs (A) and Sides (B). Nail through the Front/Backs (A) and Sides (B) into the bottom, using 1⅝-inch screws spaced every 2 inches.

Finishing

1. Sand the assembled fence planter thoroughly. An optional step is to drill several holes through the bottom of the planter, to allow the plants to drain properly.

2. Paint or stain the planter and gingerbread ornaments the colors of your choice—or leave the planter its natural color. (If you decide to paint or stain the planter and ornaments the same color, you may do so after the project is completely assembled.)

3. Attach the gingerbread ornament to the front corners of the planter, using 1-inch finish nails.

4. Attach the planter to the fence. It is a good idea to use 3½-inch wood screws, and attach the planter to both the fence and the fence post. (When the planter is full of dirt and flowers, it may be too heavy for some fences.)

Yard Light

If you entertain outside a lot, you'll appreciate adding a soft glow to an unlit portion of the yard. Add this yard light to a previously dark and unused corner, and you'll increase your useable entertaining space considerably.

Materials

2 linear feet of 2 x 8 pine

13 linear feet of 1 x 6 pine

Hardware

36 1¼" wood screws

16 2½" wood screws

Exterior light kit and exterior-
     rated electrical wire★

Notes on Materials

★Before beginning this project, check local codes concerning exterior elec-trical wiring. Make certain that all of the materials you use meet these codes and that a licensed electrician is not required for this project.

Cutting List

Code	Description	Qty.	Material	Dimensions
A	Side	4	1 x 6 pine	36" long
B	Top/Bottom	2	2 x 8 pine	7¼" long

Making the Sides

1. Cut four Sides (A) from 1 x 6 pine, each measuring 36 inches.

2. Assemble the four Sides (A), overlapping each piece in rotation, as shown in figure 1. With the four sides in position, the assembly measures 6¼ inches wide on all sides. Apply glue to the meeting surfaces, and screw all four Sides (A) along their entire length, using 1¼-inch wood screws spaced about 6 inches apart.

Adding the Top and Bottom

1. Cut two Top and Bottoms (B) from 2 x 8 pine, each measuring 7¼ inches. Label one piece "Top" and one piece "Bottom."

2. Drill a ½-inch-diameter hole through the center of the Bottom (B) to accommodate the electrical wire. Then cut a ½- x ½-inch groove from the hole to one edge of

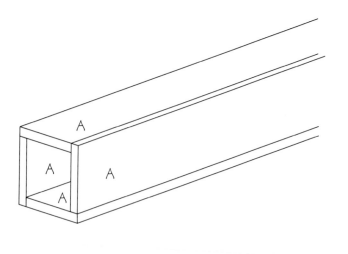

Figure 1

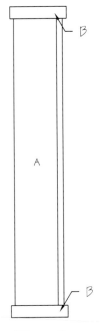

Figure 2

the Bottom (B), as shown in figure 2 (page 120). The groove will also accommodate the electrical wire and allow the finished project to sit flat.

3. Drill a hole in the center of the Top (B), and attach the exterior lamp fixture to the Top (B), following the manufacturer's directions. The size of the center hole will be determined by the type of exterior light and the installation requirements.

4. When the lamp fixture is installed, center the Top (B) over the Sides (A), making sure to place the electrical wiring inside the four Sides (A). The Top (B) should over-

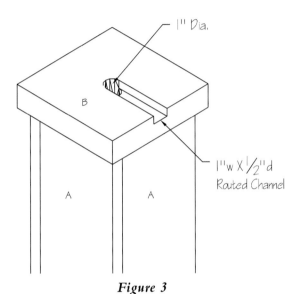

Figure 3

hang the Sides (A) by ½ inch on all sides. Apply glue to the meeting surfaces, and screw through the Top (B) into the Sides (A), using two 2½-inch wood screws on each side. (See figure 3.)

5. Insert the free end of the electrical wire through the hole on the ungrooved side of the Bottom (B), and tie a loose knot on the grooved side to make sure the wire stays in place. Center the Bottom (B) over the open end of the Sides (A). Again, the Bottom (B) should overhang the Sides (A) by ½ inch on all sides. Apply glue to the meeting surfaces, and screw through the Bottom (B) into the Sides (A), using two 2½-inch wood screws on each side.

6. Attach a plug to the end of the electrical wire, and use exterior construction glue to secure the wire inside the groove. Let the glue set up overnight.

Finishing

1. Fill all cracks, crevices, and screw holes with wood filler.

2. Stain or paint the yard light the color of your choice, or simply leave it the natural color and seal it with a waterproof finish.

Trellis and Fountain

Ah, the sound of water on a summer's day seems to cool everything down while also soothing the soul. The combination of trellis and fountain is an easy way to add a water feature to your outdoor living area without huge expense. Choose a statuary that fits in your garden and build the trellis yourself.

Materials

26 linear feet of 4 x 4 pine	
17 linear feet of 2 x 2 pine	
18 linear feet of 1 x 4 pine	
4' x 8' sheet of privacy lattice	
6 linear feet of 2 x 4 pine	

*Notes on Materials

This trellis will work with any statuary fountain piece. Most lawn and garden stores sell a variety of designs. Or you can convert a wall plaque into a fountain piece by drilling a hole through the plaque to accommodate the plastic pump hose. Be sure to purchase a pump large enough to pump the water from the tank up the height of your fountain piece. Check the pump manufacturer's specifications to be sure.

Hardware

50	2½" wood screws
20	1⅝" wood screws
30	1" wire brads
2	5" lag screws
	Fountain statuary piece★
	Fountain pump
	Plastic hose (sized to connect the statuary piece to the pump)
	Galvanized bucket, approximately 3' x 4' x 2'

Special Tools and Techniques

Miter

Cutting List

Code	Description	Qty.	Materials	Dimensions
A	Side	2	4 x 4	120" long
B	Side Supports	2	2 x 2	96" long
C	Connectors	4	1 x 4	48" long
D	Trellis	1	Lattice	4' x 8' sheet
E	Top	2	2 x 4	26" long
F	Ledge	1	4 x 4	55" long

Building the Frame

1. Cut two Sides (A) from 4 x 4 pine, each measuring 120 inches.

2. Cut two Side Supports (B) from 2 x 2 pine, each measuring 96 inches.

3. Position one Side Support (B) flush with one edge of one Side (A), as shown in figure 1. Note that the Side (A) is 4 inches from one end of the Side Support (B), and extends past the Side Support (B) 20 inches on the oppo-

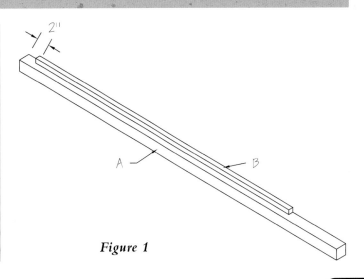

Figure 1

site end. Apply glue to the meeting surfaces, and screw through the Side Support (B) into the Side (A), using 2½-inch-long nails spaced every 5 inches.

4. Repeat step 3 to assemble a mirror image, using the remaining Side (A) and Side Support (B).

5. Cut four Connectors (C) from 1 x 4 pine, each measuring 48 inches.

6. Position the side assemblies on a level surface, 45 inches apart and parallel to each other, with the Side Supports (B) facing each other.

7. Place the one Connector (C) over the Side Supports (B), flush with the upper ends of the topmost Side Support (B), as shown in figure 2. Apply glue to the meeting surfaces, and screw through the Connector (C) into the Side Supports (B), using two 1⅝-inch wood screws on each joint.

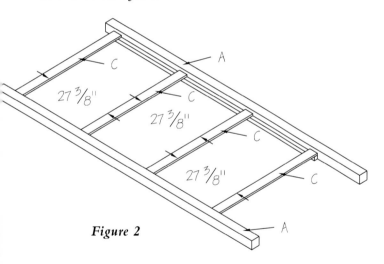

Figure 2

8. Repeat step 7 three times to attach the remaining Connectors (C), one flush with the lower end of the Side Supports (B), and the two remaining Connectors (C) in the center of the assembly, 27⅜ inches apart.

Adding the Lattice, Top, and Ledge

1. Place the 4- x 8-foot Trellis (D) on top of the four Connectors (C), as shown in figure 3. Nail through the Trellis (D) into the three connectors, using 1-inch wire brads spaced every 4 inches.

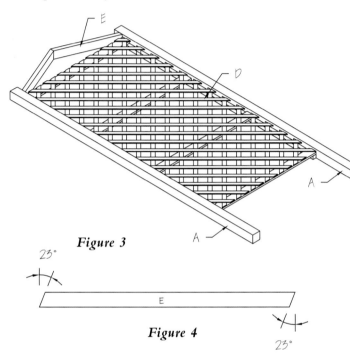

Figure 3

Figure 4

2. Cut two Tops (E) from 2 x 4 pine, each measuring 26 inches.

3. Position the Tops (E) on edge, and miter both ends of the Tops (E) at a 23° angle, as shown in figure 4.

4. Place the two Tops (E) on a flat work surface with the mitered ends together. Apply glue to the meeting surfaces, and screw through each of the Tops (E) into the opposing Top (E), using two 2½-inch finish nails on each side.

5. Using figure 3 as a guide, position the top assembly on top of the Trellis (D). Apply glue to the meeting surfaces, and screw through the ends of the Tops into the Sides (A), using two 2½-inch wood screws on each joint.

6. Cut one Ledge (F) from 4 x 4 pine, measuring 55 inches.

6. Cut one Ledge (F) from 4 x 4 pine, measuring 55 inches.

7. The Ledge (F) will be attached to the Sides (A) with two 5-inch lag screws. Predrill holes on each end of the Ledge (F) to accommodate the screws, then screw through the Ledge (F) into the Sides (A).

8. Center the fountain piece on top of the ledge, and secure the top of the fountain piece to one of the four Connectors (C). If the Connector (C) is not in the proper position for the height of your particular fountain piece, secure it to a shorter scrap piece of board placed on the opposite side of the trellis.

Finishing

1. Place the galvanized bucket on the ground beneath the fountain, then position the pump inside the bucket. Attach the plastic hose to the fountain piece. Guide the plastic hose down the back side of the Trellis (D), then back through the Trellis (D) to the front of the trellis behind the galvanized bucket.

2. Set the completed trellis in the desired outdoor location, taking care to stabilize the structure against strong winds. We placed our trellis in a corner of the yard and secured it to both sides of the fence.

3. Set the galvanized bucket at the bottom center of the trellis, fill it with water. Then connect the free end of the plastic hose to the pump.

Metric Conversion Chart

Inches	Centimeters		Inches	Centimeters
1/8	3 mm		12	30
1/4	6 mm		13	32.5
3/8	9 mm		14	35
1/2	1.3		15	37.5
5/8	1.6		16	40
3/4	1.9		17	42.5
7/8	2.2		18	45
1	2.5		19	47.5
1¼	3.1		20	50
1½	3.8		21	52.5
1¾	4.4		22	55
2	5		23	57.5
2½	6.25		24	60
3	7.5		25	62.5
3½	8.8		26	65
4	10		27	67.5
4½	11.3		28	70
5	12.5		29	72.5
5½	13.8		30	75
6	15		31	77.5
7	17.5		32	80
8	20		33	82.5
9	22.5		34	85
10	25		35	87.5
11	27.5		36	90

Index

Acknowledgments

As always, there are many people who spent many hours making this book better. We would like to take this opportunity to thank them.

Our gratitude to: Laura Dover Doran (Lark Books, Asheville, North Carolina), our editor, who tirelessly sorted through our manuscript and drawings and contributed so very much to the final book; Chris Bryant (Lark Books, Asheville, North Carolina), art director, who suffered through heat exhaustion and temporary tattoos to make sure we "got the shot"; Evan Bracken (Light Reflections, Hendersonville, North Carolina), who made it through yet another shoot with professionalism, humor, and patience; and Todd Jarrett (Sarasota, Florida), illustrator, who put together excellent illustrations in very short order.

Special thanks also to the following companies for helping with the production of this book: Intermatic, Inc. (Intermatic Plaza, Spring Grove, Illinois 60081-9698, www.intermatic.com) provided the wonderful outdoor lighting fixtures and Stanley Tools (New Britain, Connecticut 06053, www. stanleyworks.com) helped us cut, measure, and shape the projects.